Essays on L

CW00551391

MARILYN HACKER is the author of
poems, most recently *Desesperanto,*
2003. She received the Lenore Mar̲̲̲̲̲̲̲̲̲̲̲̲̲̲̲̲̲̲̲̲̲̲̲̲̲̲
American Poets in 1995 for *Winter Numbers,* which also received a
Lambda Literary Award; her *Selected Poems* received the Poets' Prize
in the United States in 1996. Her first book, *Presentation Piece,* was a
Lamont Poetry Selection of the Academy of American Poets, and
received the National Book Award the following year, 1975. She has
published several books of translations including *A Long-Gone Sun*
(Sheep Meadow Press, 2000) and *Birds and Bison* (Sheep Meadow
Press, 2004) both of poems by Claire Malroux, and *Here There Was
Once a Country* (Oberlin College Press, 2001) and *She Says* (Graywolf
Press, 2003) both by Vénus Khoury-Ghata. The former Editor in
Chief of the *Kenyon Review,* Hacker now serves on the editorial
boards of *Literary Imagination* in the United States and *Siècle 21* in
France. She received an Award in Literature from the American
Academy of Arts and Letters in 2004. Marilyn Hacker divides her
time between New York and Paris, and teaches at the City College
of New York and the CUNY Graduate Center.

MARILYN HACKER

Essays on Departure

NEW AND SELECTED POEMS

Oxford*Poets*

CARCANET

First published in Great Britain in 2006 by
Carcanet Press Limited
Alliance House
Cross Street
Manchester M2 7AQ

'In violet circles', 'Cricket hunts were also in the evening', 'It was a long week of delights beginning', 'Beauty comes from Spain', from *A Long-Gone Sun* by Claire Malroux, translated by Marilyn Hacker, published in the United States in 2000 by the Sheep Meadow Press. Poems reprinted by kind permission of the publisher. 'The Seven Honeysuckle Sprigs of Wisdom' appears in *Here There Was Once A Country*, poems by Vénus Khoury-Ghata, translated by Marilyn Hacker, published in the United States in 2001 by the Oberlin College Press Field Translation Series and reprinted by kind permission of the publisher. Of the translations of poems by Hédi Kaddour, 'The Bus Driver', 'The Scarab Bookshop' and 'Spiritual Distress' were first published in *PN Review*. 'Rue de Tournon' was first published in the *Paris Review* and appeared in the anthology *Twentieth-Century French Poems* edited by Stephen Romer (Faber & Faber, 2002). 'Six-Thirty' was first published in *Poetry*. 'Variations' was first published in *Verse*. Translations reprinted by kind permission of Hédi Kaddour. The translation of Guy Goffette's 'Four Seasons for Jude Stéfan' first appeared in *PN Review*. It was also published in *Poetry International* in the United States. Translations reprinted by kind permission of Guy Goffette. Translations of poems by Emmanuel Moses reprinted by kind permission of the author.

A CIP catalogue record for this book is available from the British Library
ISBN 1 903039 78 9
978 1 903039 78 6

The publisher acknowledges financial assistance from Arts Council England

Typeset by XL Publishing Services, Tiverton
Printed and bound in England by SRP Ltd, Exeter

Contents

Acknowledgements

The author wishes to thank the Centre National du Livre (France) for a grant which aided in the creation of this book.

New Poems
'Letter to Hayden Carruth' was published in *Poetry International* in the United States, and in the anthology *Poets Against the War*. It also appeared in *Versal* (The Netherlands). 'Glose (Storm)' was first published in *PN Review*, and in *Bloom* in the United States. It appeared in the 2006 *Pushcart Prize* anthology. 'Glose (The Year of the Dragon)' was published in *PN Review*, and in *Pleiades* in the United States. 'Ghazal: In Summer' was first published in *Plant Care*, a festschrift for Mimi Khalvati (Linda Lee Books, 2004), and in *The Walrus* in Canada. 'Letter to Mimi Khalvati' was first published in *Plant Care*, a festschrift for Mimi Khalvati (Linda Lee Books, 2004), and in *Bat City Review* in the United States. 'For Kateb Yacine' was published in *PN Review* and in the *New England Review* in the United States. It was included in the anthology *Best American Poetry 2005* (Simon & Schuster), edited by Paul Muldoon and David Lehman. 'For Anna Akhmatova' and the 'Glose' on Akhmatova's 'Willow' were commissioned for Poetry International 2004 at the South Bank Centre. 'For Anna Akhmatova' was published in *Modern Poetry in Translation*, and in *Prairie Schooner* in the United States. 'Glose' appeared in *Poetry London*. 'Ghazal: The Beloved' and 'Ghazal: Begin' were first published in *PN Review*.

from
TAKING NOTICE
(1980)

Pantoum

There is a serviceable wooden dory
rocking gently at the lip of ocean,
from where her moor line loops back loosely
to an outrider of the wet forest.

Rocking gently at the lip of ocean,
whorled and rosy carapaces glimmer.
To an outrider of the wet forest
who kneels at the undulant flat belly

whorled and rosy carapaces glimmer
under, the water is a mirror dreaming.
Who kneels at the undulant flat belly
feels her pulse gyre in the liquid circles.

Under the water is a mirror dreaming
furled leaves. She kneads and presses her friend's spine,
feels her pulse gyre in the liquid circles
her palm oils on smooth skin, opening like

furled leaves. She kneads and presses her friend's spine,
enters her own blood's tiderush, leaves
her palm oils on smooth skin. Opening like
shrubbery parting to bare fingers, she

enters. Her own blood's tiderush leaves
her charged with flammable air, igniting the
shrubbery. Parting to bare fingers, she
grows, reaches into the fire licking

her, charged with flammable air, igniting the
dry tinder, and the wet places that flame like brandy.
Grows, reaches into the fire licking
her clean, that nourishes as it consumes

dry tinder. And the wet places that flame like brandy
are knowledgeable. They affirm
her: clean. That nourishes as it consumes
detritus of self-doubt, whispers she fears

are knowledgeable. They affirm
each other in themselves. Still, when the
detritus of self-doubt whispers, she fears
the empty pool, that secret. They could lose

each other in themselves, still. When the
postcards begin arriving, they depict
the empty pool, that secret. They could lose
jobs, balance, money, central words, music.

Postcards begin arriving. They depict
themselves living in a perfect landscape, with
jobs, balance, money: central. Words, music
one made for the other, late at night, as they rocked

themselves. Living in a perfect landscape, with
passionate friends, you'd ache, she thinks.
One made for the other? Late at night, as they rocked
into incognate languages, were they still

passionate friends? You'd ache, she thinks,
if your mind buzzed with translations of denial
into incognate languages. Were they still
anywhere near the hidden rainforest?

If your mind buzzed with translations of denial,
you might not see the gapping in the hedgerows,
anywhere near the hidden rainforest,
a child could push through, or a tall woman stooping.

You might not see the gapping in the hedgerows
at first. She grew up here, points out where
a child could push through, or a tall woman. Stooping,
howevermany shoulder in, to the brambles

at first. She grew up here, points out where
the path mounts, damp under eye-high ferns.
However many shoulder into the brambles,
each one inhales the solitude of climbing.

The path mounts, damp under eye-high ferns.
Cedars aspire to vanishing point in the sky.
Each one inhales the solitude of climbing
lichenous rocks. In soft perpetual rain,

cedars aspire to vanishing point in the sky,
then, sea-stained and enormous, niched for foothold,
lichenous rocks, in soft perpetual rain.
Each, agile or clumsy, silently scales them.

Then, see: stained and enormous, niched for foothold
by tide pools sloshing broken shells and driftwood
(each, agile or clumsy, silently scales them
to her own size), boulders embrace the sound.

By tide pools sloshing broken shells, and driftwood
from where her moor line loops back loosely
to her own sides (boulders embrace the sound
there) is a serviceable wooden dory.

Feeling and Form

for Sandy Moore and for Susanne K. Langer

Dear San: everybody doesn't write poetry.
A lot of people doodle profiles, write
something they think approximates poetry
because nobody taught them to read poetry.
Rhyming or trailing gerunds, clumps of words
straggle a page, unjustified – poetry?
It's not like talking, so it must be poetry.
Before they learn to write, all children draw
pictures grown-ups teach them how not to draw.
Anyone learns/unlearns the craft of poetry
too. The fourth grader who gets a neat like-
ness of Mom in crayon's not unlike

the woman who sent you her Tone Poem, who'd like
her admiration praised. That isn't poetry,
unless she did the work that makes it like
this, any, work, in outrage, love, or lik-
ing an apple's October texture. Write
about anything – I wish I could. It's like
the still lives you love: you don't have to like
apples to like Cézanne. I do like words,
which is why I make things out of words
and listen to their hints, resounding like
skipping stones radiating circles, drawing context from text, the way I've watched you draw

a pepper shaker on a table, draw
it again, once more, until it isn't like
anything but your idea of a drawing, like an idea of movement, drawing its shape from sequence. You write poetry.
I was a clever child who liked to draw,
and did it well, but when I watch you draw,
you rubber-face like I do when I write:
chewed lip, cat-tongue, smiles, scowls that go with right
choices, perplexed, deliberate, withdrawn
in worked play, conscious of the spaces words
or lines make as you make them, without words

for instant exegesis. Molding words
around a shape's analogous to drawing these coffee cups in settings words
describe, but whose significance leaves words
unsaid, because it's drawn, because it's like
not my blue mug, but inked lines. Chosen words
– I couldn't write *your white mug* – collect words
they're meant, or drawn to, make mental space poetry
extends beyond the page. If you thought poetry
was merely nicely ordered private words
for two eyes only, why would you say, 'Write
me a letter, damn it!' This is a letter, right?

Wrong. Form intimates fiction. I could write
me as a mathematician, weave in words
implying *you* a man, sixteen, a right-
handed abstract expressionist. I'd write
untruths, from which some other *you* could draw
odd inferences. Though I don't, I write
you, and you're the Donor on the right-
hand panel, kneeling in sable kirtle. Likely I'm the lady left of you, who'd like
to peer into your missal, where the writing (legible Gothic) lauds in Latin poetry
the Lady at the center. Call her poetry,

virtual space, or Bona Dea. Poetry
dovetails contradictions. If I write
a private *you* a public discourse, words
tempered and stroked will draw you where you draw
these lines, and yours, convergent, made, unlike:

that likelihood draws words I write to poetry.

from
ASSUMPTIONS
(1985)

from *Open Windows*

3

for Sára Karig

On the back of a letter in French applying
for a place in a bilingual school for my daughter,
I put words that will not contain the slaughter
of somebody's twenty-year-old. She is dying
under a modern airport where the roar
of takeoffs flattens screams and retching to blurred
industrial noise around the torturer.
Beneath the tiled floor is the dirt floor.
A woman is living whose name I say like a charm
because she acknowledged choice in the dulled eyes
of somebody's son, who, needled to recognize
a congruent soul in the law student or farm
child he is reducing to an integer
of shamed pain, would be stripped and killed with her.

4

While deathdrunk superannuated boys
tot up how often to blow up the world
a white-locked pink sage with a toddler voice
recounts, purse clutched, how she was blued and curled.
I overhear her on the crosstown bus
I take at three to meet the second grade.
She smiles a smile someone called dangerous
once, and she boiled it down like marmalade.
I'm sheared, hands free, with keys, jackknife and ten
dollars deployed in worn corduroy pants.
A matrifocal world would comprehend
compassion, dignity, and common sense,
I sneer, aware of my accoutrements
as she is, talking hairdos with her friend.

7

for Eunice Gutman (Río de Janeiro)

'How come, here, you see so many black
people working in other people's houses?'
Does she notice, every other friend of ours is
ambiguous two generations back?
Like Bedouin for *sand*, or Eskimo
for *snow*, mixed races swell the lexicon,
peach-cream through copper to obsidian:
preta, negrinho, mulata, moreno.
Her café-au-lait father, olive mother
made her *rubia*, gold on lion-gold,
like the naked sungilt three-year-old
who, crouched near a bloat sewer, ferreted
his hillside of the disinherited,
looking enough like her to be her brother.

8

for Nélida Piñion

'How come,' she says, 'if you were what she is,
District Attorney, and someone did what
you thought they had a reason for, you've got
to say they're guilty? If you have the same ideas?
That boy – how could somebody say he is
going to learn anything in jail? He shot
the father 'cause he hurt his sister, not
to kill him!' Our polyglot host, child-free, is
charmed by such eloquence so late at night.
Iva waits, in Portuguese, to get
her lasagna. 'It doesn't *taste* right.'
The waiter brings a more familiar heap.
Stretching her four-foot-six on the banquette,
swiftly and righteously, she falls asleep.

10

Now that she reads in bed till ten P.M.,
she does by the dim pillow-lamps of hotel
rooms in old towns whose names she cannot spell,
with walls around, churches centering them.
She won't go in museums, but will scale
any Romanesque or Gothic pile,
racing term-end outings of French school-
children sharing stretched possibles: a real
duke's birdcage dungeon straddling the south tower,
the sacristan's maquette beyond the bell
of vineyards, dollhouse fortress on a hill,
shadowed by pensive monsters who aspire
to the Lady's intercessive smile
as boats head slowly elsewhere up-canal.

11

Vence

She marched away, tagged 'Unaccompanied Minor,'
and idiotically, I felt like weeping,
although I didn't get any work done for
two weeks, except mornings while she was sleeping
late, her round brown face through dirty hair
clear as a Koré's, and for once not talking.
I tried to scribble at the town pool where
she swam, fair days or foul. Incessant walking
up steep hills on the back streets firmed up my
calves, lengthened my wind, and kept my blood-pressure
down. I needn't eat only where pizza
is served, or stockpile Limonade and Treets – a
slight recompense. French kids on holiday
will hog the pool, and already I miss her.

Graffiti from the Gare Saint-Manqué

for Zed Bee

Outside the vineyard is a caravan
of Germans taking pictures in the rain.
The local cheese is Brillat-Savarin.
The best white wine is Savigny-les-Beaune.
We learn Burgundies while we have the chance
and lie down under cabbage-rose wallpaper.
It's too much wine and brandy, but I'll taper
off later. Who is watering my plants?
I may go home as wide as Gertrude Stein
– another Jewish Lesbian in France.

Around the sculptured Dukes of Burgundy,
androgynous monastics, faces cowled,
thrust bellies out in marble ecstasy
like child swimmers having their pigtails toweled.
Kids sang last night. A frieze of celebrants
circles the tomb, though students are in school,
while May rain drizzles on the beautiful
headlines confirming François Mitterand's
election. We have Reagan. Why not be
another Jewish Lesbian in France?

Aspiring Heads of State are literate
here, have favorite poets, can explain
the way structuralists obliterate
a text. They read at night. They're still all men.
Now poppy-studded meadows of Provence
blazon beyond our red sardine-can car.
We hope chairpersons never ask: why are
unblushing deviants abroad on grants?
My project budget listed: Entertain
another Jewish Lesbian in France.

I meant my pithy British village neighbor
who misses old days when sorority
members could always know each other: they wore
short-back-and-sides and a collar and tie.
She did, too. Slavic eyes, all romance
beneath an Eton crop with brilliantined
finger-waves, photographed at seventeen
in a dark blazer and a four-in-hand:
a glimpse of salad days that made the day for
another Jewish Lesbian in France.

Then we went on to peanuts and Campari,
she and her friend, my friend and I, and then
somehow it was nine-thirty and a hurry
to car and *carte* and a carafe of wine,
Lapin Sauté or Truite Meunière in Vence.
Convivial quartet of friends and lovers:
had anyone here dreaded any other's
tears, dawn recriminations and demands?
Emphatically not. That must have been
another Jewish Lesbian in France.

It's hard to be almost invisible.
You think you must be almost perfect too.
When your community's not sizeable,
it's often a community of two,
and a dissent between communicants
is a commuter pass to the abyss.
Authorities who claim you don't exist
would sometimes find you easy to convince.
(It helps if you can talk about it to
another Jewish Lesbian in France.)

A decorated she-Academician
opines we were thought up by horny males.
No woman of equivalent position
has yet taken the wind out of her sails.
(How would her 'lifelong companion' have thanked her?)
Man loving Man's *her* subject, without mention
if what they do is due to her invention
– and if I'd been her mother, I'd have spanked her.
(Perhaps in a suppressed draft *Hadrian*'s
another Jewish Lesbian in France.)

Then the advocates of Feminitude
– with dashes as their only punctuation –
explain that Reason is to be eschewed:
in the Female Subconscious lies salvation.
Suspiciously like Girlish Ignorance,
it seems a rather watery solution.
If I can't dance, it's not my revolution.
If I can't think about it, I won't dance.
So let the ranks of *Psych et Po* include
another Jewish Lesbian in France.

I wish I had been packed off to the nuns
to learn good manners, Attic Greek, and Latin.
(No public Bronx Junior High School fit all that in.)
My angsts could have been casuistic ones.
It's not my feminist inheritance
to eat roots, drink leaf broth, live in a cave,
and not even know how to misbehave
with just one vowel and five consonants.
This patchwork autodidact Anglophone's
another Jewish Lesbian in France,

following Natalie Barney, Alice B.
Toklas, Djuna Barnes, generous Bryher,
Romaine Brooks, Sylvia Beach, H.D.,
Tamara de Lempicka, Janet Flanner.
They made the best use of the circumstance
that blood and stockings often both were bluish;
(they all were white, and only Alice Jewish)
wicked sept / oct / nonagenarians.
Would it have saved Simone Weil's life to be
another Jewish Lesbian in France?

It isn't sex I mean. Sex doesn't save
anyone, except, sometimes, from boredom
(and the underpaid under-class of whoredom
is often bored at work). I have a grave
suspicion ridicule of Continence
or Chastity is one way to disparage
a woman's choice of any job but marriage.
Most of us understand what we renounce.
(This was a lunchtime peptalk I once gave
another Jewish Lesbian in France

depressed by temporary solitude
but thinking coupled bliss was dubious.)
I mean: one way to love a body viewed
as soiled and soiling existential dross
is knowing through your own experience
a like body embodying a soul
to be admirable and loveable.
That is a source that merits nourishment.
Last night despair dressed as self-loathing wooed
another Jewish Lesbian in France.

The sheet was too soft. Unwashed for three weeks,
it smelled like both of us. The sin we are
beset by is despair. I rubbed my cheeks
against the cotton, thought, I wouldn't care
if it were just *my* funk. Despair expands
to fill ... I willed my arm: extend; hand: stroke
that sullen shoulder. In the time it took
synapse to realize abstract commands,
the shoulder's owner fell asleep. Still there
another Jewish Lesbian in France

stared at the sickle moon above the skylight,
brooding; equally sullen, that alone
is better after all. As close as my right
foot, even my bed stops being my own.
Could I go downstairs quietly, make plans
for myself, not wake her? Who didn't undress,
slept on the couch bundled with loneliness
rather than brave that nuptial expanse
five weeks before. Another contradiction
another Jewish Lesbian in France

may reconcile more gracefully than I.
We're ill-equipped to be obliging wives.
The post office and travel agency
are significant others in our lives.
Last summer I left flowers at Saint Anne's
shrine. She had daughters. One who, legends tell,
adrift, woman-companioned, shored (is still
revered) in the Camargue, her holy band's
navigatrix, Mary, calming the sea
– another Jewish Lesbian in France?

It says they lived together forty years,
Mary and Mary and Sarah (who was black).
Unsaintly ordinary female queers,
we packed up and went separately back.
We'd shared the road with Gypsy sleeper vans
to join Sarah's procession to the shore.
Our own month-end anabasis was more
ambiguous. Among Americans
my polyglot persona disappears,
another Jewish Lesbian in France.

Coeur mis à nu in sunlight, khaki pants
I've rolled up in a beach towel so ants
and crickets from the leafage won't invade
their sweaty legs: in a loaned hermit-glade
pine-redolent of New Hampshire, not France,
I disentangle from the snares I laid.
Liver-lobed mushrooms thicken in the shade,
shrubs unwrap, pinelings thrust through mulch. Noon slants
across my book, my chest, its lemonade
rays sticky as a seven-year-old's hands.

Part of a True Story

for Margaret Delany

We dress UP!

Ntozake Shange

My dear Mrs. Bloomer:
                              The exigencies
of my life demand rational costume.
I noticed recently upon perusal
of a number of your interesting
journal, *The Lily*, that your radical
bifurcate garment for gentlewomen
is beyond suggestion; not to mince words,
for sale.
            My people, Mrs. Bloomer, are
as well, south of the District, and until
the last and least of us no longer is
chattel, this woman must be radical
to be rational. A woman of color
is gentle as yourself, until provoked.
I have been, since the age of six.
                                          When I,
aged twenty-some, returned to the scene
of my truncated childhood, with the goal
– which I achieved – of bringing forth my mother
and my father from bondage, as I had
my brothers, many of my sisters and
brothers, I was obliged, for my safety
and theirs, to come to them in male attire.
(Does *attire* have gender?) I cannot pass
as other than I am in one respect;
nor would I wish to. It was curious
passing that other way, where I had passed
before: 'This gal can haul as heavy a
load as three men or a mule,' et cetera.
A black man is only marginally
more anonymous on a southern road
than a black woman. Dare I confess, I
liked that marginal anonymity?
Crop-headed in a neutral suit of clothes,

I sat, a stranger at my mother's table,
bearing good news she could not bear to hear
who bore me, till I bared myself as well,
scarred as I was, to loving scrutiny.
Later, I also bore the scrutiny
of the spouse whom I had reluctantly
left; who, free, had forbidden me to go
to freedom. Newly wived, he did not know
me at all, either as woman or as
myself. It's a peculiar thing: to pass
easily, anonymously, from one
life, or mode of life, to another: done
with a forked suit? Night, starvation, a gun
to scare stragglers to courage, sleep in snow
or straw or not at all are what I know
as passage rites. I do what I can,
but I do not wish to be thought a man
again.
            Tonight, four hundred human souls,
still embodied, disembondaged, lie wakeful
or sleep in this rough but hospitable
hospice, this time, taken across water
to free land. You know the name I am called.
The straits do not. We cross them nonetheless.
I have another name now: General;
a task I had first as a nursling: Nurse.
We intend to bring out four hundred more.
I wish to be there. It is efficacious
that I be there. I must be recognized
though: black, female, and old, or nearly old.
Still, I am of scant use immobilized.
I wish to be relieved of the woolen gown
whose waterlogged skirts and underskirts hold
me so, as well as the Confederate
Army would wish. I was nearly drowned.
Thus, Mrs. Bloomer, my request. Disguise
is not wished, or called for. Compromise,
though unaccustomed, is appropriate
on this occasion. So is the connection
of our aims. I entertain reflection
that, free and black, I am still disfranchised,
female; a condition I first realized
espoused: bondwoman and freedman, we

embodied it. I transcend limitation.
I am a black woman, whose education
was late and little: necessity
of adulthood vowed to emancipation
of my people; the larger limitation
imposed by childhood spent in servitude,
leave me comparatively unlettered.
You will receive this missive, dictated
by me to my adjutant, from her
hand, to which I pray you will deliver
the costume I desire.

Awaiting your
kind reply, I remain,

Yours faithfully,

Harriet Tubman   United States Army
Medical Division   Port Royal Island

Port Royal Island was captured from the Confederacy by the Union Army in 1861 and became a haven for escaped slaves. Harriet Tubman, then aged about forty-one, and the most successful – and hunted – conductor on the Underground Railroad, was sent there by the governor of Massachusetts in 1862. She served as an Army scout and as a nurse and herbal healer in the field hospital established for the freed slaves and wounded soldiers. In 1863, she led a detachment of the Second South Carolina Volunteers, a company composed of black soldiers under the command of Colonel James Montgomery, in a raid up the Combahee River, with the objectives of destroying the torpedoes with which the Confederate Army had mined the river, and of liberating as many slaves from the coastal farms as could be transported to Port Royal on the gunboats. More than eight hundred were freed. Harriet Tubman thus added the sobriquet 'General' to the name of Moses, by which even her commanding officer addressed her.

Shortly afterward, Tubman, who had never learned to read and write, dictated a letter to Boston, ordering a Bloomer suit, because long skirts were a handicap on such a campaign.

Amelia Bloomer, feminist, abolitionist, and originator of the costume which bore her name, was also editor of *The Lily*, a periodical advocating women's rights.

I'd like to express my gratitude to Ann Petry for her biography of Harriet Tubman; its concise information fueled my imagination.

Rune of the Finland Woman

for Sára Karig

'You are so wise,' the reindeer said, 'you can bind the winds of the world in a single strand.'

H.C. Andersen, 'The Snow Queen'

She could bind the world's winds in a single strand.
She could find the world's words in a singing wind.
She could lend a weird will to a mottled hand.
She could wind a willed word from a muddled mind.

She could wend the wild woods on a saddled hind.
She could sound a wellspring with a rowan wand.
She could bind the wolf's wounds in a swaddling band.
She could bind a banned book in a silken skin.

She could spend a world war on invaded land.
She could pound the dry roots to a kind of bread.
She could feed a road gang on invented food.
She could find the spare parts of the severed dead.

She could find the stone limbs in a waste of sand.
She could stand the pit cold with a withered lung.
She could handle bad puns in the slang she learned.
She could dandle foundlings in their mother tongue.

She could plait a child's hair with a fishbone comb.
She could tend a coal fire in the Arctic wind.
She could mend an engine with a sewing pin.
She could warm the dark feet of a dying man.

She could drink the stone soup from a doubtful well.
She could breathe the green stink of a trench latrine.
She could drink a queen's share of important wine.
She could think a few things she would never tell.

She could learn the hand code of the deaf and blind.
She could earn the iron keys of the frozen queen.
She could wander uphill with a drunken friend.
She could bind the world's winds in a single strand.

ESSAYS ON DEPARTURE

The Little Robber Girl Gets On in the Wide World

for Julie Fay

She's in a room full of letters, dressed in white
amidst proliferate papers, the exploded lace of sheets.
Her hair froths white, her pale eyes chill, as when I first
saw her. Under white trouser legs, her long feet

are bare on the stone floor, swollen with heat.
Summer follows summer since the first time
I stood in her crepuscular bedroom
awaiting acknowledgment. The dim chime

of a blue glass clock caught her attention. 'I'm
exhausted. Come at six tomorrow. Knock
downstairs. I'll hear you. The heat makes me sick.
Debarrass me of that ridiculous clock.'

I put it in my pocket. I left the lock
unlatched. Who knows what I thought I'd do?
I watched from a huge-boled olive tree, her window
a tall candle, while dusk deepened, blue

as my road clothes, and a blade of new
moon sharpened above the limestone bluffs.
'I knew where you were last night. I heard you laugh.'
Her sight is dim, but her ears are sharp enough.

I thought, 'Let her be captious, she's a tough
old bird, and, say what you like, she deserves
a bit of courtesy. While I'm here, I won't starve.
You're not a slave when you contract to serve.'

I don't know when it was I lost my nerve.
I was delighted when she seemed to trust
me. I brought the right coins back, her birdscratch list
transformed to fill the larder. Late in the August

heat, shadowed by shutters, we discussed
my future and her past. Sometimes they blended
to one chivalric tale. I understand it
a little better now. She would make splendid

generous gestures in which I pretended
to believe. If it were hers to give,
she'd give it to me – what? her land, her glove
to carry, the bracelet under her sleeve?

Pretended? Why? She didn't want me to leave;
she told me so in several languages,
while I continued to sleep under her trees,
presenting myself mornings, neatly dressed

as I could manage. Each day was a new test.
She sent me out and always I came back
with packages, messages. 'You bring me good luck.'
I had good luck, I thought. I had a knack

for pleasing. The blue glass clock lived in my rucksack.
Afternoons, I wrote letters, a diligent steward,
weeded the moribund garden while it parched,
stood barefoot on cool tiles while she descended

the tortuous stairway, her gnarled hand extended
toward me. Did I say, she was beautiful,
that youth, in her scintillant pallor, paled
to decorative nursery pastel?

I felt large, rude and bland, all the more grateful,
though my food and outdoor shelter were all my wages.
Blackberry clumps weighted the brambly hedges.
Sometimes I thought of winter hills' blank pages

scrawled with one bird track. I forgot my real age – is
that strange? and that once I was almost always cold.
Brown rabbits and gray water rats ran wild
in the hedges. No animal should be killed

on her land, she said. My nights outdoors were filled
with rustlings, scrabblings. I thought about rats
and rolled down, shivering, into my blankets.
'Womanish,' she mocked, when I told her that.

I plunged my face into a fresh-washed sheet
as I lifted it to hang. The odor
of wet linen enveloped unthought-of tears.
I never had done woman's work before

but now I did it daily, over and over.
Sometimes I was insulted, as no servant
who'd take her pay and leave would be. I didn't.
Sometimes I was her twilight confidante,

gallant, or granddaughter, or sycophant.
She liked me best when I was brusque and lewd.
If I was timid, she would call me stupid,
but she'd laugh and correct a misconstrued

sentence I almost halfway understood.
The sun set earlier, but we sat late. Around her
shoulders, I wrapped her black-barred cloak. She was fonder
of talk than fire. Meanwhile the magpies, sometimes the thunder,

meanwhile the footpath wound serpentine under
the bushes, tucked in around limestone boulders
above the river-sectioned slopes where wilder
things wandered in the night as I got older,

and she, chameleon, stayed the same, I told her.
Meanwhile the trail debouched on a small road
that led – although I didn't know where it led –
somewhere. From our hill, it was hidden by woods.

After a storm, mist marked the bluffs: it showed.
Meanwhile I scrabbled weeds where no one reaped.
Harvest was windfall. Greengages the wasps
ate splattered tree roots, or heaped

in their forks, a rats' feast while we slept.
Smashed yellow pears fermented in the grass
the afternoon I thought I'd cut my losses.
With a soiled shirt sleeve, I rubbed the milk-glass

clock till my face glimmered back from its facets.
I wrapped my four garments around it, rolled
them in my blanket. I stripped her down-drowned bed
of its champagne-silk crewelwork. I sold

that to a market woman. Well, I thought of it, told
myself I ought, might, was entitled to,
as I tied up the rucksack. *Do you know,*
that's probably what she expects of you?

So I turn, part hedges, shield my eyes. I go
up to my haunches in persistent brambles.
Nobody promised me it would be simple.
Nobody's future passes out free samples.

Sunbeams stroked me at a farewell angle
while the watchlight in my mind's eye sought her
shadow smiting rock with an olive crosier:
'You are a thief, and a thief's daughter!'

Ballad of Ladies Lost and Found

for Julia Álvarez

Where are the women who, *entre deux guerres*,
came out on college-graduation trips,
came to New York on football scholarships,
came to town meeting in a decorous pair?
Where are the expatriate *salonnières*,
the gym teacher, the math-department head?
Do nieces follow where their odd aunts led?
The elephants die off in Cagnes-sur-Mer.
H. D., whose 'nature was bisexual,'
and plain old Margaret Fuller died as well.

Where are the single-combat champions:
the Chevalier d'Eon with curled peruke,
Big Sweet who ran with Zora in the jook,
open-handed Winifred Ellerman,
Colette, who hedged her bets and always won?
Sojourner's sojourned where she need not pack
decades of whitegirl conscience on her back.
The spirit gave up Zora; she lay down
under a weed field miles from Eatonville,
and plain old Margaret Fuller died as well.

Where's Stevie, with her pleated schoolgirl dresses,
and Rosa, with her permit to wear pants?
Who snuffed Clara's *mestiza* flamboyance
and bled Frida onto her canvases?
Where are the Niggerati hostesses,
the kohl-eyed ivory poets with severe
chignons, the rebels who grew out their hair,
the bulldaggers with marceled processes?
Conglomerates co-opted Sugar Hill,
and plain old Margaret Fuller died as well.

Anne Hutchinson, called witch, termagant, whore,
fell to the long knives, having tricked the noose.
Carolina María de Jesús'
tale from the slag-heaps of the landless poor
ended on a straw mat on a dirt floor.
In action thirteen years after fifteen
in prison, Eleanor of Aquitaine
accomplished half of Europe and fourscore
anniversaries for good or ill,
and plain old Margaret Fuller died as well.

Has Ida B. persuaded Susan B.
to pool resources for a joint campaign?
(Two Harriets act a pageant by Lorraine,
cheered by the butch drunk on the IRT
who used to watch me watch her watching me.)
We've notes by Angelina Grimké Weld
for choral settings drawn from the *Compiled
Poems* of Angelina Weld Grimké.
There's no such tense as Past Conditional,
and plain old Margaret Fuller died as well.

Who was Sappho's protégée, and when did
we lose Hrotsvitha, dramaturge and nun?
What did bibulous Suzanne Valadon
think about Artemisia, who tended
to make a life-size murderess look splendid?
Where's Aphra, fond of dalliance and the pun?
Where's Jane, who didn't indulge in either one?
Whoever knows how Ende, Pintrix, ended
is not teaching Art History at Yale,
and plain old Margaret Fuller died as well.

Is Beruliah upstairs behind the curtain
debating Juana Inés de la Cruz?
Where's savante Anabella, Augusta-Goose,
Fanny, Maude, Lidian, Freda and Caitlin,
'without whom this could never have been written'?
Louisa who wrote, scrimped, saved, sewed, and nursed,
Malinche, who's, like all translators, cursed,
Bessie, whose voice was hemp and steel and satin,
outside a segregated hospital,
and plain old Margaret Fuller died as well.

Where's Amy, who kept Ada in cigars
and love, requited, both country and courtly,
although quinquagenarian and portly?
Where's Emily? It's very still upstairs.
Where's Billie, whose strange fruit ripened in bars?
Where's the street-scavenging Little Sparrow?
Too poor, too mean, too weird, too wide, too narrow:
Marie Curie, examining her scars,
was not particularly beautiful;
and plain old Margaret Fuller died as well.

Who was the grandmother of Frankenstein?
The Vindicatrix of the Rights of Woman.
Madame de Sévigné said prayers to summon
the postman just as eloquent as mine,
though my Madame de Grignan's only nine.
But Mary Wollstonecraft had never known
that daughter, nor did Paula Modersohn.
The three-day infants blinked in the sunshine.
The mothers turned their faces to the wall;
and plain old Margaret Fuller died as well.

Tomorrow night the harvest moon will wane
that's floodlighting the silhouetted wood.
Make your own footnotes; it will do you good.
Emeritae have nothing to explain.
She wasn't very old, or really plain –
my age exactly, volumes incomplete.
'The life, the life, will it never be sweet?'
She wrote it once; I quote it once again
midlife at midnight when the moon is full
and I can almost hear the warning bell
offshore, sounding through starlight like a stain
on waves that heaved over what she began
and truncated a woman's chronicle,
and plain old Margaret Fuller died as well.

from

LOVE, DEATH AND THE CHANGING OF THE SEASONS

(1986)

Runaways Café I

You hailed a cab outside the nondescript
yuppie bar on Lexington to go
downtown. Hug; hug: this time I brushed my lips
just across yours, and fire down below
in February flared. O bless and curse
what's waking up no wiser than it was.
I will not go to bed with you because
I want to very much. If that's perverse,
there are, you'll guess, perversions I'd prefer:
fill the lacunae in: one; two; three; four ...
I did, cab gone. While my late bus didn't come,
desire ticked over like a metronome.
For you, someone was waiting up at home.
For me, I might dare more if someone were.

Runaways Café II

For once, I hardly noticed what I ate
(salmon and broccoli and Saint-Véran).
My elbow twitched like jumping beans; sweat ran
into my shirtsleeves. Could I concentrate
on anything but your leg against mine
under the table? It was difficult,
but I impersonated an adult
looking at you, and knocking back the wine.
Now that we both want to know what we want,
now that we both want to know what we know,
it still behooves us to know what to do:
be circumspect, be generous, be brave,
be honest, be together, and behave.
At least I didn't get white sauce down my front.

Wagers

I bet you don't wear shoulder pads in bed.
I bet when we get over, we'll be *bad!*
I bet you blush all over when you come.

Although the butch coach gave them out, and said,
they're regulation issue for the team,
I bet you don't wear shoulder pads in bed;

and if I whispered something just unseem-
ly enough, I could make your ears turn red.
I bet you blush all over when you come

to where I say, I slept on what we did,
and didn't, then undressed you in a dream.
I bet you don't wear shoulder pads in bed.

I bet my blue pajamas split a seam
while I thought of my hand on you instead.
I bet you blush all over when you come.

Maybe I'll spend Bastille Day feeling bad,
deferring fireworks till the troops get home
– I bet you don't wear shoulder pads in bed.

Don't give me any; just promise me some.
I'm having nicer nightmares than I had.
I bet you blush all over when you come,

but I can bide my time until it's bid-
dable (though, damn, you make me squirm;
I bet you don't wear shoulder pads in bed),

wait till the strawberries are ripe for cream,
and get to give, for having kept my head.
I bet you blush all over when you come.
I bet you don't wear shoulder pads in bed.

'O little one, this longing is the pits.'

O little one, this longing is the pits.
I'm horny as a timber wolf in heat.
Three times a night, I tangle up the sheet.
I seem to flirt with everything with tits:
Karyn at lunch, who knows I think she's cute;
my ex, the D.A. on the Sex Crimes Squad;
Iva's gnarled, canny New England god-
mother, who was my Saturday night date.
I'm trying to take things one at a time:
situps at bedtime, less coffee, less meat,
more showers, till a remedy appears.
Since there's already quite enough Sex Crime,
I think I ought to be kept off the street.
What are you doing for the next five years?

'Well, damn, it's a relief to be a slut'

Well, damn, it's a relief to be a slut
after such lengths of 'Man delights not me,
nor woman neither,' that I honestly
wondered if I'd outgrown it. Chocolate
or wine, a cashmere scarf, a cigarette,
had more to do with sensuality
than what's between my belly and my butt
that yearns toward you now unabashedly.
I'd love to grip your head between my thighs
while yours tense toward your moment on my ears,
but I'll still be thankful for this surprise
if things turn out entirely otherwise,
and we're bar buddies who, in a few years,
will giggle about this after two beers.

'Didn't Sappho say her guts clutched up like this?'

Didn't Sappho say her guts clutched up like this?
Before a face suddenly numinous,
her eyes watered, knees melted. Did she lactate
again, milk brought down by a girl's kiss?
It's documented torrents are unloosed
by such events as recently produced
not the wish, but the need, to consume, in us,
one pint of Maalox, one of Kaopectate.
My eyes and groin are permanently swollen,
I'm alternatingly brilliant and witless
– and sleepless: bed is just a swamp to roll in.
Although I'd cream my jeans touching your breast,
sweetheart, it isn't lust; it's all the rest
of what I want with you that scares me shitless.

'Though sometimes now we sound like fiancées'

Though sometimes now we sound like fiancées
curmurring futures that augment like growths,
I've never touched you underneath your clothes,
or seen you more than twice in seven days.
I venture it's a trifle premature
to sign the china-pattern registry
before you are, at least, at liberty
to hang your PJ's on my bathroom door.
A funny pair of homebodies we are,
as wicked as we like to paint ourselves:
I kiss you till my clit's about to burst,
and catch myself reorganizing shelves.
Let's go to some disreputable bar
and do a little fancy dancing first.

What You Might Answer

'I'm going to do what *I* want just this once!
Plums dropped in laps are often overripe.
I don't eat liver, and I won't eat tripe.
Nobody needs her Frye boots cast in bronze.
I don't like crowds, and now I'm feeling crowded.
I can speak tongues, but not the ones your friends
gossip with you about me in. The end's
still moot, jackboots. I have to think about it.
Two yards of hair, two miles of legs – and she
is also who's, for years, seen what I've seen.
We both need to be twenty-five years old.
You want a masturbation fantasy?
Some girls you know put out a magazine
full of them – but I'm not the centerfold.'

Eight Days in April

1

I broke a glass, got bloodstains on the sheet:
hereafter, must I only write you chaste
connubial poems? Now that I have traced
a way from there to here across the sweet-
est morning, rose-blushed blonde, will measured feet
advance processionally, where before
they scuff-heeled flights of stairs, kicked at a door,
or danced in wing-tips to a dirty beat?
Or do I tell the world that I have got
rich quick, got lucky (got laid), got just what
the doctor ordered, more than I deserved?
This is the second morning I woke curved
around your dreaming. In one night, I've seen
moonset and sunrise in your lion's mane.

2

Moons set and suns rise in your lion's mane
through LP kisses or spread on my thighs.
Winter subsided while I fantasized
what April dawns frame in the windowpane.
Sweetheart, I'm still not getting enough sleep,
but I'm not tired, and outside it's spring
in which we sprang the afternoon shopping
after I'd been inside you, O so deep
I thought we would be tangled at the roots.
I think we are. (I've never made such noise.
I've never come so hard, or come so far
in such a short time.) You're an exemplar
piss-elegance is not reserved for boys.
Tonight we'll go out in our gangster suits.

3

Last night we went out in our gangster suits,
but just across the street to Santerello's,
waited past nine for wine. We shone; the fellows
noticed. 'You have a splendid linen coat,'
Dimitri told you as he sat us down.
(This used to be my local; now it's chic.)
A restaurant table's like a bed: we speak
the way we do calmed after love, alone
in the dark. There's a lot to get to know.
We felt bad; we felt better. Soon I was
laid back enough to drink around the bend.
You got me home, to bed, like an old friend.
I like you, Rachel, when you're scared, because
you tough it out while you're feeling it through.

4

You tough it out while you're feeling it through:
sometimes the bed's rocked over tidal waves
that aren't our pleasures. Everyone behaves
a little strangely when they're in a new
neighborhood, language, continent, time zone.
We got here fast; your jet lag's worse than mine.
I only had Paris to leave behind.
You left your whole young history. My own
reminds me to remind you, waking shaken
with tears, dream-racked, is standard for the course.
We need accommodation that allows
each one some storage space for her dead horse.
If the title weren't already taken,
I'd call this poem 'Directions to My House.'

5

I'd call this poem 'Directions to My House,'
except today I'm writing it in yours,
in your paisley PJs. The skylight pours
pale sunlight on white blankets. While I douse
my brain with coffee, you sleep on. Dream well
this time. We'll have three sets of keys apiece:
uptown, downtown, Paris on a sublease.
Teach me to drive. (Could I teach you to spell?)
I think the world's our house. I think I built
and furnished mine with space for you to move
through it, with me, alone in rooms, in love
with our work. I moved into one mansion
the morning when I touched, I saw, I felt
your face blazing above me like a sun.

6

Your face blazing above me like a sun-
deity, framed in red-gold flames, *gynandre*
in the travail of pleasure, urgent, tender
terrible my epithalamion
circles that luminous intaglio
– and you under me as I take you there,
and you opening me in your mouth where
the waves inevitably overflow
restraint. No, no, that isn't the whole thing
(also you drive like cop shows, and you sing
gravel and gold, are street-smart, book-smart,
laugh from your gut) but it is (a soothing
poultice applied to my afflicted part)
the central nervous system and the heart.

7

The central nervous system and the heart,
and whatever it is in me wakes me
at 5 A.M. regardless, and what takes me
(when you do) ineluctably apart
and puts me back together; the too-smart,
too-clumsy kid glutted on chocolate cakes (me
at ten); the left-brain righteousness that makes me
make of our doubled dailiness an art
are in your capable square hands. O sweet,
possessives make me antsy: we are free
to choose each other perpetually.
Though I don't think my French short-back-and-sides
means I'll be the most orthodox of brides,
I broke a glass, got bloodstains on the sheet.

'Five-thirty, little one, already light'

Five-thirty, little one, already light
outside. From Spanish Harlem, sun spills through
the seamless windows of my Gauloise blue
bedroom, where you're sleeping, with what freight
of dreams. Blue boat, blue boat, I'll navigate
and pilot, this dawn-watch. There's someone who
is dying, darling, and that's always true
though skin on skin we would obliterate
the fact, and mouth on mouth alive have come
to something like the equilibrium
of a light skiff on not-quite-tidal waves.
And aren't we, when we are on dry land
(with shaky sea legs) walking hand in hand
(often enough) reading the lines on graves?

'How can you love me with the things I feel'

How can you love me with the things I feel
that scare me crashing on the window glass?
How can you love me when I'm such an ass-
hole (sometimes) I can't take hold of what's really there and use it, let you take the wheel
and put my head back as the truck-stops pass?
Where would we go that morning? Would the grass
beside the highway mount to granite, steel
and rubber take us far enough that I
could pull my ghosts out of my guts and cry
for them, with you behind me, on some high
stone place, where water breaks from underground
arteries with hard breaths, that would sound
like mine, letting them go, saying good-bye?

'Grief, and I want to take it up in you;'

Grief, and I want to take it up in you;
joy, and I want to spend it all inside
you; fear, and you are the place I can hide.
Courage is what leaves me brave enough to
turn you around and tell you what to do
to me, after. Rivers, and downstream glide
I; we breathe together. You look, or I'd
get scared, but you're watching while you take me through
the deep part, where I find you, where you need
to know I do know where, know how to drive
the point home. Wit: you get the point and flat
statement of a gift of tongues. I get
up, and you get me down, get lost, you lead
me home, or I take you, and we both arrive.

It was the best week ever, but...

Remind me of what's coming, not what's past.
I've got five closets full of souvenirs:
secondhand shirts and linens I amassed

in Languedoc last summer, Iva's cast-
off bluejeans (the French dress she wore two years
reminds me of what's coming, not what's past),

Raggedy Ann, some Lincoln Logs, a vast
stuffed lion, one stretch-suit from Mothercare,
secondhand shirts and linens I amassed

when she was new in London. There's bombast-
ic Berlioz her dad abandoned there.
Remind me of what's coming, not what's past.

I guess you know, although you haven't asked,
if ever you need shelf space, it's to spare:
secondhand shirts and linens I've amassed

can be culled through, a closet emptied fast
for your chiaroscuro winter gear.
Remind me of what's coming, not what's past –

though we need both: our two fall birthdays, last
week in Paris, Sundays when we wear
secondhand shirts, and linens we've amassed

get rumpled by our matinal bareassed
pastimes, while our private jokes, our queer
secondhand shirts, and linens we've amassed
remind us of what's coming, by what's past.

La Loubiane

Two long-haired women in the restaurant
caress each other's forearms. I avert
my eyes. I'm glad to see them there; I hurt
looking on, lonely, when I so much want
to touch your arm, your hand like that, in front
of two *mémés* enjoying their dessert,
a British couple with two kids, alert
their girls are pigging *frites*, and me. I can't,
and wouldn't, let them know: I'm one; it makes
my thoughts real when they touch each other. They're
guests at the hotel. They go in through
the glassed-in terrace, slow upstairs, to view
the moon go down through snarled vines of their hair.
The little English girls devour their cakes.

Letter on August 15

Warm wind tumbles the washing on the line,
blow-drying it at twice a dryer's speed.
    I'm here; you're not.
If no one made this maxim up, it's mine:
    The less you have, the less you need.
Nobody misses what they haven't got

a clue to. (I've never longed for a car,
and the Vençois don't miss a laundromat.)
    I long for you
the livelong day, and all night long. You are
    I know, worth going on about
– knowledge which, at the moment, doesn't do

me any good. Someone who's lifted weights
for months, then quits, finds that sinuous force
    soon turns to flab.
My fiber's sagging now. Back in the States
    you miss me too. That makes it worse.
You'd drop downstairs by twos and hail a cab

and come uptown, if I were home uptown.
More prudently, I'd take the bus to Nice's
    flower-bed airport,
wave from the deck while the Airbus touched down,
    then, there you'd be. Now the breeze is
transmitting a late-afternoon report

of birdshot on the bluffs of the Malvan,
with cries of men and dogs, and (elsewhere) babies.
    Assumption Day
had morning market, so good mothers can
    lay out the feast. Not risen, they, dec-
ently clad, brought extra francs to pay

for a tall, thin white candle or a squat
one in a cup, this morning, before Mass.
    In Paris, you
lit them, twice, for your father, joking that
    Mary was tolerant, would pass
over, quicker than he, your bad Hebrew.

I lit one for my mother, awkwardly,
today – the squat kind; I'm more used to tapers –
    and thought of her,
Sonny Wainwright, and Catherine Karolyi.
    At the Régence, with newspapers
in French and English, I fancied you were

feeding me crossword clues from the *Tribune*,
saying my sugarless *citrons pressés*
    were *dégueulasses*.
I walked back to my hermitage at noon,
    washed out some shirts, and spent the day's
hot hours under the pine trees where the grass

under their fragrant sheddings can't grow much.
I sat on a straw beach-mat with James Wright
    and the blue sky,
and, salted down with sweat, wished I could touch
    you now with words, that cooler night
breezes would touch us both, that there'd be eye

contact and talk across a dinner table.
You might not like the half-mile walk uphill
    to restaurants,
shops and cafés. One day, I may be able
    to smile as you appraise the vil-
las and old-age pensioners of Vence.

I imagine your one, Florida mother
drinking pastis here, midday, with her peers,
    gilt middle-class
emigrées. In New Jersey, the other,
    who's seen you once, in twenty years,
may have thought about you today at Mass,

as I did, without sacraments, your rings'
unspecified contract on my left hand
     meaning as big, or
as small, a thing as how we'll manage things.
     Your large soul's from that Jewish man;
that Irish woman fueled its hybrid vigor,

then left you knowing just enough to miss
a scent, a texture – where the memory
     lives, you forget.
She is, for ignorance of what she is,
     the obvious banality
of corner boys' most frequent epithet.

Can we fill out each other's family?
My child (missing you can't obliterate
     how I've missed her)
is cagey, but confided in you, she
     had measured out our three birthdates
and liked that you could be her older sister

– which makes me feel like everybody's aunt,
wishing to cast spinsterly ironies on
     my August quandary
of wanting you here with me, where you can't
     be, anyway, not this season.
The sun is dropping. I'll take in the laundry.

'On your birthday, I reread Meredith,'

On your birthday, I reread Meredith,
whose life's mean truths inform, tonight, his text
so generously framed. There'll be the next
night, and the next, cold gaps. I'd have been with
you now, lover and friend, across the width
of some candle-lit table as we mixed
habit and hope in toasts. Instead, perplexed
by separation like a monolith
bulked in the rooms and hours I thought would be
ours, I practice insensibility.
We crossed four miles, three thousand. You diminish
now, on a fogged horizon, far away.
Your twenty-fifth was our first class Tuesday
– will one year bracket us from start to finish?

'Will one year bracket us from start to finish,'

Will one year bracket us from start to finish,
who, in an evening's gallant banter, made
plans for new voyages to span decades
of love and work around a world we'd win? Wish
was overgrown with fears; voyages vanish
with empty wine bottles and summer's paid
bills. Lengthens the legendary blade
between us: silence; hope I hope to banish;
doubt, till I almost doubt what happened, did.
Chicken from Zabar's warms, and frozen spinach
simmers, while Iva writes a school essay:
'Both Sides: Everything has an opposite ...'
sucking her inky fingers and her braid,
and I read Meredith, on your birthday.

from
GOING BACK TO THE RIVER
(1990)

Nights of 1962
The River Merchant's Wife

for Carol Lee Hane

Emigrée from the Bronx, a married child
hit the ghetto-turned-barrio, making wild
conjectures and conjunctions, making wrong
turns on lyrics of country-and-western songs.
Moondark to dawn, loud streets were not-quite-scary
footnotes in a nocturnal dictionary
of argot softer on my ears than known
four-walled cadenzas to: the night alone,
the day on fire. (My age, the boss boy knew.)
From Avenue C west to Sixth Avenue
and Eighth Street, I'd aim for the all-night Whelan's,
eat solo ham and eggs. The night sky paled, sands
into the river's timer. One more day:
jeans switched for dark dress, tight shoes, the subway
to work at Altman's. Five months short of twenty,
I knocked back whatever the river sent. He
was gone two days; might bring back, on the third,
some kind of night music I'd never heard:
Sonny the burglar, paunched with breakfast beers;
olive-skinned Simon, who made fake Vermeers;
the cardsharp who worked club cars down the coast;
Carol, stone butch, who'd booked Chip's group, was host,
bouncer, bookkeeper, and night manager
of a folk club. The night she spotted her
sometime girlfriend naked in my red chalk
drawings taped to the john wall, we had a talk
about how she bridged night's work and day's work,
a dude till dawn, a nine-to-five file clerk
in heels and hose. Some grass: she demonstrated
her butch walk, girl walk, paced, like a five-gaited
horse, the splintered floor, miming her cross-
over from flunky to three A.M. yard boss.
Fox-faced in burnt sienna, the judge's daughter
ignored us. Was it Carol who had bought her
the watch she left on, posing, to keep time?
I learned the lesson as a paradigm
of living day-life, night-life, Janus-faced.

Why didn't Carol, older, have her own place?
Where did she sleep the nights she didn't crash
on our spare mattress at East Fifth Street? Cash
she stored in the front pocket of her drip-
dry chinos, which she slept *on*, laid out under
the mattress for their knife-edge. Who, I wondered,
did she sleep *with*, now? She'd told things to Chip
she wouldn't tell me, who'd only (she'd guess) botched
stoned fumblings while somebody's boyfriend watched.
I knew the boys' bars – did she go to one
for girls? I dawdled nights on the question.
Two weeks later: what did they make of me
on a barstool at the Sea Colony
in a paint-splattered Black Watch shirt, old khak-
i work pants, one long braid straight down my back,
chain-smoking Camels, making my second Bud
last? I sipped it as slowly as I could,
looking around me surreptitiously.
Boys' bars had dance floors. Puerto Rican queens
in mohair sweaters, who'd worked up routines
in kitchens, line-danced to 'No Milk Today,'
'From a Jack to a Queen,' 'Walk Like a Man,'
too cool to giggle at the *double enten-
dres*, cruising without seeming to cruise.
No one was dancing here. Women in twos,
each suit-and-tie paired with a plunge-necked sheath,
held hands at tiny tables, closed. Bad teeth
and Brooklyn accents, nineteen-year-old snob
thought, in the wrong outfit for either job
– and how invade with chat hermetically
sealed couples? Somebody romantically
forty-plus, foreign, solitary, face
defined by facing danger, in this place
for R & R, who'd like my mind, whose bed,
dovetailed by bookshelves, was four blocks away ...
Seduction by the French Department head
to whom I owed a paper on Genet
was what I had in mind, and I assumed
she'd know how to proceed beyond the full-
face closeup kiss on which my mind's lens zoomed
in, blanked out. I should have followed Carol
on her night off. She knew the regulars,
I guessed. I couldn't sit on a barstool

reading, till closing. Chip had adventures;
I, it seemed, had trepidations. Full
of them, I got down the rest of my beer
and turned tail, out the door into the night
streets, which aroused just reasonable fear.
I lengthened my strides streetlight to streetlight,
in no hurry to regain the empty
conjugal crash pad and wait out the dregs
of the dark. I was, I told myself, hungry
enough to hit Whelan's for ham and eggs.

Torch

Pillar of sequins in a Saturday-
night club, or did she bob in Alice Faye
Peter Pan collar to the microphone,
cradle it, while she mooned at him, and croon
fifties kitsch, but clean as a plain gold ring?
He liked to hear her sing. She liked to sing.
Twenty-seven to his forty-four,
ex-cashier and rag-trade entrepreneur,
both smoked like gangsters, downed good Scotch, closed bars.
So does their daughter, who keeps three guitars
for late-night chord changes in a dim room,
and has stood up behind a podium.
Why did the red-headed torch singer quit
the spotlight, spouse, their child? It doesn't fit.
However she puts pieces together
all she has left is the one who left her
fair hair, a Celtic temper, a torch song
and a walk-out. She also started young.

Riposte

(I never could
Figure out how anyone can justify poetry
As a full-time job. How do they get through
The day at MacDowell — filling out
Applications for the next free lunch?)
                    Tom Disch, 'Working on a Tan'

Dear Tom,
            When my next volume (granted: slender)
is granted an advance of more than two
thou, perhaps I'll scorn all grants and spend a
couple of them on summer rent, like you,

in the right Hampton with the novelists
who swap Hollywood options with bravado.
Their *au pairs* hoard handwritten shopping-lists;
their word-processors go with them to Yaddo

where novelists are still *persona grata*,
nor do their royalties or last advance
cause the *per diem* charge to rise *pro rata*.
I'd ever so much rather be in France

and not have to eat dinner at six-thirty
with frozen carrots and Kraft's French (*sic*) Dressing.
But potshotting 'free-lunch' is playing dirty;
successful applicants should count their blessings.

I wouldn't want the kitchen staff to brand me
an ingrate who will bite the hand that feeds me
if I am going to eat the food they hand me
— and they're in the minority that reads me.

Is poetry a full-time occupation?
Practitioners have spliced it with exciting
alternative careers in transportation
— drive cabs, that is — or teach Creative Writing

or First-Year French or Freshman Composition,
translate, wait tables, sell insurance, edit.
If 'poet' 's written where it says: PROFESSION,
American Express extends no credit.

And you see no excuse for poets' lives
because we're paid so mingily; that's it?
I think of 'unemployed' mothers, housewives
whose work was judged equivalent to shit-

shoveling on Frank Perdue's chicken farm
by gents who calibrate Job Equity.
All that they are today they owe to Mom!
Do novelists owe shit to poetry?

SF writer snipes poets on the pages
of *Poetry*: that's also aiming low,
though nowhere near as low as poets' wages.
At fifty cents a line, where would *you* go?

And fifty cents a line's exemplary!
Measure it to your last *Playboy* short-short
and you might find an artists' colony
a perfectly respectable resort.

Cultural Exchanges

for Catherine Tinker

When Augusta, the teenaged *empleada*,
expressed bewilderment at the two friends'
behavior, 'Oh, they're North Americans,'
the *Doña* said, implying that explained
everything. She stretched out, with the telephone
parked on the zipper of her overalls.

Message-pad leaves were scattered over all
the desks and shelves. This house's *empleada*
primarily answered the telephone.
Half the time it was her hometown friends
with city jobs, now, too. 'No,' she explained,
she wasn't working for Americans

– a single woman. The Americans
wanted her conversations over. All
day they hung around her. (She could have explained
the courtesies owed to an *empleada*.
They were sloppier than her brother's friends!)
In fact, they hung around the telephone.

One of them always had to telephone
someone. She didn't think North Americans
visiting *ought* to have so many friends.
Some afternoons small groups came over, all
middle-class women, with an *empleada*
working at home. They set her down, explained

she could listen, too, while they explained
why women – 'Augusta! Get the telephone!' –
were all one class, *Doña* and *empleada*.
They had – 'Translate, someone. The Americans …'
petitions to circulate over all
the neighborhoods, they hoped she'd show her friends,

to make abortion legal. (Her best friend's
midwife aunt did that, but never explained.)
They showed a film she wished was over. All
that blood! She snuck out, to the telephone
in the study. There, the Americans,
not bickering now, groped and sighed amply. Ada,

her friend, was the group leader's *empleada*.
She telephoned. Could she stay over? All
night? Like the Americans, she explained.

Going Away from the River

Midsummer's Eve: rain slants into docked barges
near the Jardin des Plantes. Cut your losses.

Soon the inhabitants will leave the city
to the international monoglot young.

Out of the smallest, oldest perched village
branch well-marked paths, beside the stream, the ravine.

The streams flow down into the local river.
The footpaths widen into roads back here.

I lived upriver from a different harbor.
Let's say: the boat left without me.

Two altos braided the Drinking Gourd.
Then there was only one voice in the dark.

In October when the fog comes down
early, the moorings are invisible.

Hard to distinguish one old duffel bag,
see the ravine, the rock-path up from dockside.

The highway spared the hill town it bypassed.
I can still get there, leave there, overland.

Les Serpillières

To my upstairs writing-table, to hers downstairs:
crash of the long plank shelf above the stove.

The casserole voided its simmering *poule
au pot*, spending its juices on the tiles.

A jar of capers broke, a jar of curry, a jar of honey.
The kitchen flags reeked: some exotic stew.

She in her loose blue jumper, I in my loose blue shorts
stood, horrified, outside the kitchen doorway,

then she scooped the chicken into the pot;
I dived under the sink for *serpillières*:

squares of soap-roughened cotton fiber, one apiece.
Scouring the corners of our refectory

we gathered honeyed shards of broken glass,
scooped up mounds of capers, herbs and honey.

'*Les serpillières!* My unlamented marriage!
How he loved to see me on my knees!'

My mother never called them '*serpillières*'
but for hours, after work, she scrubbed floors with them.

'If I'd been alone when that thing came down
I'd have sat on the floor with it and cried!'

'I would have, too – but neither of us were.'
One at the lavabo, one at the kitchen basin,

we each washed and wrung a *serpillière*,
hung them on the line outside to dry.

Market Day

Today is the *jour de marché*
downhill from Nullepart-sur-Colline.
In white voile for the heat of the day,
the secondhand Benetton jeans,

downhill from Nullepart-sur-Colline,
I take the goatpath through the woods.
The secondhand Benetton jeans
ward off horseflies and gnats, as they should.

I take the goatpath through the woods
till the narrow *ruelles* to the square
ward off horseflies and gnats. As they should,
with baskets, the *bonnes ménagères*

till the narrow *ruelles* to the square,
precede me to cherries and bread.
With baskets, the *bonnes ménagères*
are *aïeules*, behind and ahead.

Precede me to cherries and bread
in communion you shared before I did.
Our *aïeules* behind and ahead,
your grandmothers, students, were guided

in communion you shared before I did,
annealing the task to the leisure.
Your grandmothers' students were guided:
'woman's work' may include woman's pleasure.

Annealing the task to the leisure,
I pick a live trout for my dinner.
Woman's work may include woman's pleasure –
if I were a little bit thinner.

I pick a live trout for my dinner
with a few leaves of wintergreen *blettes*.
If I were a little bit thinner,
what delicious confections I'd get:

with a few leaves of wintergreen *blettes*
and cheese, are made heavenly pies.
What delicious confections I'd get
at the *fripes*, if I'd shave down one size!

(But the cheese! and the heavenly pies!)
I can figure out all the Swiss labels
at the *fripes*, if I shave down one size
from French in the heaps on the tables.

I can figure out all the Swiss labels,
but the Languedoc twang's pretty far
from French. In the heaps on the tables,
buried under the *polyestère*

(but the Languedoc twang's pretty far
down in) are mauve silk and beige cotton.
Buried under the *polyestère*,
surpassing the treasures I've gotten

down in, are mauve silk and beige cotton
for the lives that I wish that I led.
Surpassing the treasures I've gotten
in my time, there's a hoard in my head.

For the lives that I wish that I led
have these garments, these victuals as staples.
In my time, there's a hoard in my head
to be laid out on college-ruled paper.

Have these garments, these victuals, as staples
the transformative substance required
to be laid out on college-ruled paper
like a loaf brushed with gold for the fire?

The transformative substance required:
a coin in the hand of the maker.
Like a loaf? Brushed with gold from the fire,
ranked according to size by the bakers.

'A coin in the hand of the maker!'
The Romany weaver of baskets,
ranked according to size by the baker's
snacking biscuits, pursues me to ask it.

The Romany weaver of baskets
– while her daughters tend wares as they laugh,
snacking biscuits – pursues me to ask: 'It's
made to last! Will you take it for half?'

While her daughters tend wares, as they laugh,
one counts change, one is plaiting new reeds,
made to last. 'Will you take it for half?'
Now it's here, filled with things that I need.

One counts change, one is plaiting new reeds,
in white voile for the heat of the day.
Now it's here, filled with things that I need:
today is the *jour de marché*.

Celles

for Julie Fay

We liked its name, those ones, feminine plural.
We imagined the abandoned village
inhabited by sisters and sororal

friends, restoring walls and foliage.
Each house could have a window on the lake,
that now were ruins on the shore, a pillaged

battleground, the site of an earthquake
softened by bushes like a cemetery?
Evacuated by decree, to make

a giant oxbow where there was a valley.
The water licked the town's limits, and stopped.
The town was saved from drowning, but kept empty.

One evening's rhythms let us interrupt
a drive toward dinner in Lodève, to swerve
down where a gouged raw path made an abrupt

plunge to the water, following the curve
of red clay foothills. Mississippian.
to test your four-wheel drive, or test your nerve,

you said when we were safely parked. The sun
glared behind the windshield, gilt the swells
of water. We got out. Your Indian

print dress blew back around you; your hair fell
glowing across your throat. 'You ought to be
painted like that, the patron saint of *Celles*

qui vagabondent autour d'une autre vie.'
Scrub oak reclaimed what once was the café.
Swallows swooped through what once was the *mairie*,

banked into a thermal, veered halfway
across the water, toward a thicketed
dusk-dappled hill, then back, elegant play

of gliders celebrant above our heads,
spiraling in the current's arabesque.
'If we were the evacuees,' you said,

'it wouldn't be so fucking picturesque
to live in Clermont in an HLM.
They were the last ones anybody asked

'if making up this place was good for them
And we are making them up, just as much
as sorceresses flocked here for the name.'

We made our way through nascent underbrush
to climb the mayor's ragweed-shattered stairs.
Elbow to elbow, though we didn't touch,

we stood on the wind-littered terrace, where
we watched the sun continue its descent.
We drove away before it disappeared

leaving Those Ones lapped by revenant
shadows, now the cicadas' choral
song broke for nightfall, leaving Celles silent
like us, feminine plural, transient.

Dinner with Elizabeth

'The iron doors opened on a gallery.
Unshaven soldiers in shirtsleeves were playing cards.

There was a light from a few exhausted candles.
Had I seen this before? Was it a painting?

It was nearly four o'clock in the morning.
It occurred to me: this is happening to me.'

The wine came. She tasted it, and sent it back,
in a tobacco cloud. She is eighty-four.

'We set up a dormitory for the foundlings
in the ballroom of the borrowed villa.

They took shifts with us on the barricades.
The children who had guns slept with their guns.

We piled the guns in the middle of the ballroom
where they could all see them. Then they could all sleep.

Can you find your way back home from here?'
She left Vermont for Paris fifty years,

four wars ago. I am a Bronx Jew
whose leasehold names me resident for two.

Separate Lives

The last time I talked to you in my head
was July third, 1986,
in Paris. It was four A.M. A slick
Brazilian singer at Bercy instead
of dinner, last train home. The unmade bed
reproached me, and the lamp I had to fix
whose feeble current threw a ghostly flick-
er up and down the pages as I read,
a contrapuntal subordinate clause
to every sentence. Starting to dogear
my page in *Souvenirs Pieux*, I told
you what and why I thought of Yourcenar,
then blubbered out loud like a six-year-old
'Come home!' although I didn't know where that was.

If you'd gone home, I didn't know where that was
– not uptown, Languedoc, or the Marais
for you, wherever you were. All that day
I'd checked off errands that a person does
at home. Six months before, I'd wept across
just about every street in the *troisième*.
I felt like a surveyor marking them
with snot and tears. Home is where work and loss
intersect until they feel like life.
I lived on that street for as many seasons
as I had lived with you. Nobody's wife
clocked the barges in through harbor grass.
A hard-on has no conscience. Neither has
heartbreak. I didn't want to know your reasons.

Hard break I didn't want: to know your reasons
couldn't have made it easier, or could
it? A good cry beats a rotten mood.
Too good; too bad: she scared herself. Now she's on
her own, third person singular. No *frissons*
transforming verbs whose 'thou' is understood.
Half through the night, almost out of the 'would
she hear me testifying on my knees on
this not entirely metaphoric floor'
phase, I wasn't wondering who you were
when, why, where, whether we – no, you – were gone
into the winter when the deejays spun
'You have no right / to ask me how I feel.'
As if I'd died and lived to tell the tale.

And if I'd died and lived to tell the tale,
recovered from the knowledge I'd recover,
I looked a little less like death warmed over.
Mist fingering the windowpane of pale
dawn wasn't a ghost child tapping 'Fail,'
or, if she was, I wasn't frightened of her.
Morning would find me indisposed to suffer
through haunted coffee reading shadow mail:
the letter forwarded two months too late,
the sonnet sequence in a magazine
which wasn't, though it might have been, about
the face on facing page not facing mine,
the Wite-Out in the next-to-the-last line,
the message on your answering machine.

The message on your answering machine
was 'Wing it,' – something like 'Go, fly, be free.'
I chinked my dime through the cacophony
of Twenty-third and Sixth. It played again.
That was the week of leftovers and mean
songs. You'd asked to borrow back your key.
You probably were where you said you'd be.
You probably wouldn't have let me in.
Then Friday night was Sunday afternoon,
the time I didn't know was the last time
you took me in your mouth and made me come,
you took your looseleaf, and a cab downtown.
Now a phone call costs more than a dime.
There were some changes in the interim.

There were some changes in the interim
since you left, since I ran out of tears,
since I ran into you after three years.
The corners of your eyes, behind pale-rimmed
glasses are wet, flood, meltdown. My hands trem-
ble now, yours too. It's cold as hell in here.
The private parts I have between my ears
fill up when words slow down and handle them,
but I'm too close to home to need a ride.
I don't know if you have the words I need.
I know you didn't need the ones I had.
Would it have come out better than it did
if I had played it on the other side,
if I had shut the book and understood?

If I had shut the book and understood
I'd reached the end of *Souvenirs Pieux*
whose subtext was a dialogue with you
in absentia, and 'gone for good'
just the return address when you replied,
I might have grieved for grief. I only knew
I'd finished crying, and there was a blue-
gray hint of day above the slate outside,
a lunch date about seven hours away.
You've brought me back a book, past grief, half known,
still strange, with your name on it, not the one
I wrote, for me to open where you say
things for yourself, that aren't what you said
the last time I talked to you in my head.

Nights of 1964–1966
The Old Reliable

for Lewis Ellingham

The laughing soldiers fought to their defeat ...
James Fenton, 'In a Notebook'

White decorators interested in Art,
black file clerks with theatrical ambitions,
kids making pharmaceutical revisions
in journals Comp. instructors urged they start,
the part-Cherokee teenage genius (maybe),
the secretary who hung out with fairies,
the copywriter wanting to know, where is
my husband? the soprano with the baby,
all drank draft beer or lethal sweet Manhattans
or improvised concoctions with tequila
in summer when, from Third Street, we could feel a
night breeze waft in whose fragrances were Latin.
The place was run by Polish refugees:
squat Margie, gaunt Speedy (whose sobriquet
transliterated what?). He'd brought his play
from Lódź. After a while, we guessed Margie's
illiteracy was why *he* cashed checks
and *she* perched near the threshold to ban pros,
the underage, the fugitive, and those
arrayed impertinently to their sex.
The bar was talk and cruising; in the back
room, we danced: Martha and the Vandellas,
Smokey and the Miracles, while sellers
and buyers changed crisp tens for smoke and smack.
Some came in after work, some after supper,
plumage replenished to meet who knew who.
Behind the bar, Margie dished up beef stew.
On weeknights, you could always find an upper
to speed you to your desk, and drink till four.
Loosened by booze, we drifted, on the ripples
of Motown, home in new couples, or triples,
were back at dusk, with IDs, at the door.
Bill was my roommate, Russell drank with me,
although they were a dozen years my seniors.

I walked off with the eighteen-year-old genius
– an Older Woman, barely twenty-three.
Link was new as Rimbaud, and better looking,
North Beach bar *paideon* of doomed Jack Spicer,
like Russell, our two-meter artificer,
a Corvo whose *ecclesia* was cooking.
Bill and Russell were painters. Bill had been
a monk in Kyoto. Stoned, we sketched together,
till he discovered poppers and black leather
and Zen consented to new discipline.
We shared my Sixth Street flat with a morose
cat, an arch cat, and pot plants we pruned daily.
His boyfriend had left him for an Israeli
dancer; my husband was on Mykonos.
Russell loved Harold, who was black and bad,
and lavished on him dinners 'meant for men'
like Escoffier and Brillat-Savarin.
Staunch blond Dora made rice. When she had
tucked in the twins, six flights of tenement
stairs they'd descend, elevenish, and stroll
down Third Street, desultory night patrol
gone mauve and green under the virulent
streetlights, to the bar, where Bill and I
(if we'd not come to dinner), Link, and Lew,
and Betty had already had a few.
One sweat-soaked night in pitiless July,
wedged on booth benches of cracked Naugahyde,
we planned a literary magazine
where North Beach met the Lower East Side Scene.
We could have titled it *When Worlds Collide*.
Dora was gone, 'In case the children wake up.'
Link lightly had decamped with someone else
(the German engineer? Or was he Bill's?).
Russell's stooped *vale* brushed my absent makeup.
Armed children spared us home, our good-night hugs
laissez-passer. We railed against the war.
Soon, some of us bused south with SNCC and CORE.
Soon, some of us got busted dealing drugs.
The file clerks took exams and forged ahead.
The decorators' kitchens blazed persimmon.
The secretary started kissing women,
and so did I, and my three friends are dead.

Elevens

There is one story and one story only …
Robert Graves, 'To Juan at the Winter Solstice'

James A. Wright, my difficult older brother,
I'm in an airplane over your Ohio.
Twice a week, there and back, I make this journey
to Cincinnati.

You are six books I own and two I borrowed.
I'm the songs about the drunk on the runway
and leaving your lover for the airport, first
thing in the morning.

You were fifty-two when you died of cancer
of the tongue, apologist for the lonely
girls who were happened to near some bleak water.
Tell me about it.

When my father died young, my mother lost it.
I am only three years younger than he was.
The older brother and the younger brother
that I never had

died young, in foreign cities, uncomforted.
Does anybody not die uncomforted?
My friend Sonny had her lovers around her
and she died also.

Half drunk on sunlight in my second country,
I yearned through six-line stanzas I learned from you.
You spent January of your last winter
up on that mountain.

I love a boy who died and a girl who left.
I love a brother who is a grown woman.
I love your eight books. I hate the ending.
I never knew you.

You knew a lot about airports and rivers
and a girl who went away in October.
Fathers, brothers and sisters die of cancer:
still, we are strangers.

You are the lonely gathering of rivers
below the plane that left you in Ohio;
you are the fog of language on Manhattan
where it's descending.

Going Back to the River

for K.J.

Dusk, iridescent gasoline floats on the
rain-puddles, peacock feathers on macadam.
    Schoolgirl beneath an awning pulls her
    collar up, here comes her bus. She's gone now.

Nine-thirty, and there's light behind thunderheads.
Storm over, in an hour it will rain again.
    Meal done, across the street a neighbor
    shakes out her tablecloth from the window.

I have a reading lamp and an open book.
Last glass of wine, last morsel of Saint-André
    prolong my dinner and my chapter
    into the ten o'clock Haydn program.

What will I say to you when I write to you?
(What would I say to someone who isn't you?)
    I'm home, I've cleaned the kitchen, taken
    charge of my solitude, taken long baths.

What do I tell myself when I open and
write in the notebook keeping me company?
    Don't stay indoors tomorrow morning.
    Do the week's shopping at Sunday market.

Go to the river, take what it offers you.
When you were young, it guarded and promised you
    that you would follow other rivers
    oceans away from a landlocked childhood.

Yes, I indulge myself in hyperbole
since I'm not going out for a walk in this
    wet weather, though I'd walk from someone
    else's place, stop on the bridge, look over.

Seine, Thames and Hudson (sounds like a publisher):
one river flows down into another one.
    Where did I sit and read alone, who
    walked with me which afternoon, which evening?

There was a river when I was leaving you.
That morning, with our *café con leche*, we
    slouched on a bench above the Hudson,
    washed in the wind of a near departure.

Not rupture: each one went where she had to go.
Still, I'd be hours and borders away from you.
    We bluffed like adolescent soldiers
    at the significant bridge or crossroad.

'Your father,' you said, 'would have been proud of you.'
'My mother never would have imagined it.'
    Poor Jews in an antagonistic
    city, they pulled in their walls around them.

One city would have looked like another one:
hard work, a clean house, food without seasoning.
    Scrub Europe from a neutral palate,
    blend and assimilate, mistrust strangers,

know in an instant which are the *lanzmänner*.
No Yiddish pet names, gossip or baby talk.
    Brownshirts outside the door would pass on
    innocent, bland Mid-Atlantic Standard.

from GOING BACK TO THE RIVER   71

Is any accent that safely nondescript?
Their child, I bruise my brain on two languages
   (neither the one they lost) four decades
   after they earned me this freedom, passing

as what they weren't: rooted American.
Their daughter, I come home to two continents,
   live with my roots tied up in parcels,
   still impecunious, maybe foolish.

Another child of children of immigrants
(Russian, Italian), you've chosen languages
   written in symbols meant to have no
   country of origin, color, gender

(though every symbol's chiseled with history).
There, you are learning chemical formulae:
   meals on the run, a book you started
   months ago under the bed, abandoned.

Life's not forever, love is precarious.
Wherever I live, let me come home to you
   as you are, I as I am, where you
   meet me and walk with me to the river.

from
WINTER NUMBERS
(1994)

Against Elegies

for Catherine Arthur and Melvin Dixon

James has cancer. Catherine has cancer.
Melvin has AIDS.
Whom will I call, and get no answer?
My old friends, my new friends who are old,
or older, sixty, seventy, take pills
with meals or after dinner. Arthritis
scourges them. But irremediable night is
farther away from them; they seem to hold
it at bay better than the young-middle-aged
whom something, or another something, kills
before the chapter's finished, the play staged.
The curtains stay down when the light fades.

Morose, unanswerable, the list
of thirty- and forty-year-old suicides
(friends' lovers, friends' daughters) insists
in its lengthening: something's wrong.
The sixty-five-year-olds are splendid, vying
with each other in work-hours and wit.
They bring their generosity along,
setting the tone, or not giving a shit.
How well, or how eccentrically, they dress!
Their anecdotes are to the point, or wide
enough to make room for discrepancies.
But their children are dying.

Natalie died by gas in Montpeyroux.
In San Francisco, Ralph died
of lung cancer, AIDS years later, Lew
wrote to me. Lew, who, at forty-five,
expected to be dead of drink, who, ten
years on, wasn't, instead, survived
a gentle, bright, impatient younger man.
(Cliché: he falls in love with younger men.)
Natalie's father came, and Natalie,
as if she never had been there, was gone.
Michèle closed up their house (where she
was born). She shrouded every glass inside

– mirrors, photographs – with sheets, as Jews
do, though she's not a Jew.
James knows, he thinks, as much as he wants to.
He hasn't seen a doctor since November.
They made the diagnosis in July.
Catherine is back in radiotherapy.
Her schoolboy haircut, prematurely gray,
now frames a face aging with other numbers:
'stage two,' 'stage three' mean more than 'fifty-one'
and mean, precisely, nothing, which is why
she stares at nothing: lawn chair, stone,
bird, leaf; brusquely turns off the news.

I hope they will be sixty in ten years
and know I used their names
as flares in a polluted atmosphere,
as private reasons where reason obtains
no quarter. Children in the streets
still die in grandfathers' good wars.
Pregnant women with AIDS, schoolgirls, crack whores,
die faster than men do, in more pain,
are more likely than men to die alone.
And our statistics, on the day I meet
the lump in my breast, you phone
the doctor to see if your test results came?

The earth-black woman in the bed beside
Lidia on the AIDS floor – deaf, and blind:
I want to know if, no, how, she died.
The husband, who'd stopped visiting, returned?
He brought the little boy, those nursery-
school smiles taped on the walls? She traced
her name on Lidia's face
when one of them needed something. She learned
some Braille that week. Most of the time, she slept.
Nobody knew the baby's HIV
status. Sleeping, awake, she wept.
And I left her name behind.

And Lidia, where's she
who got her act so clean
of rum and Salem Filters and cocaine
after her passing husband passed it on?
As soon as she knew
she phoned and told her mother she had AIDS
but no, she wouldn't come back to San Juan.
Sipping *café con leche* with dessert,
in a blue robe, thick hair in braids,
she beamed: her life was on the right
track, now. But the cysts hurt
too much to sleep through the night.

No one was promised a shapely life
ending in a tutelary vision.
No one was promised: if
you're a genuinely irreplaceable
grandmother or editor
you will not need to be replaced.
When I die, the death I face
will more than likely be illogical:
Alzheimer's or a milk truck: the absurd.
The Talmud teaches we become impure
when we die, profane dirt, once the word
that spoke this life in us has been withdrawn,

the letter taken from the envelope.
If we believe the letter will be read,
some curiosity, some hope
come with knowing that we die.
But this was another century
in which we made death humanly obscene:
Soweto El Salvador Kurdistan
Armenia Shatila Baghdad Hanoi
Auschwitz. Each one, unique as our lives are,
taints what's left with complicity,
makes everyone living a survivor
who will, or won't bear witness for the dead.

I can only bear witness for my own
dead and dying, whom I've often failed:
unanswered letters, unattempted phone
calls, against these fictions. A fiction winds
her watch in sunlight, cancer ticking bone
to shards. A fiction looks
at proofs of a too-hastily finished book
that may be published before he goes blind.
The old, who tell good stories, half expect
that what's written in their chromosomes
will come true, that history won't interject
a virus or a siren or a sealed

train to where age is irrelevant.
The old rebbetzin at Ravensbrück
died in the most wrong place, at the wrong time.
What do the young know different?
No partisans are waiting in the woods
to welcome them. Siblings who stayed home
count down doom. Revolution became
a dinner party in a fast-food chain,
a vendetta for an abscessed crime,
a hard-on market for consumer goods.
A living man reads a dead woman's book.
She wrote it; then, he knows, she was turned in.

For every partisan
there are a million gratuitous
deaths from hunger, all-American
mass murders, small wars,
the old diseases and the new.
Who dies well? The privilege
of asking doesn't have to do with age.
For most of us
no question what our deaths, our lives, mean.
At the end, Catherine will know what she knew,
and James will, and Melvin,
and I, in no one's stories, as we are.

Nearly a Valediction

You happened to me. I was happened to
like an abandoned building by a bull-
dozer, like the van that missed my skull
happened a two-inch gash across my chin.
You were as deep down as I've ever been.
You were inside me like my pulse. A new-
born flailing toward maternal heartbeat through
the shock of cold and glare: when you were gone,
swaddled in strange air I was that alone
again, inventing life left after you.

I don't want to remember you as that
four o'clock in the morning eight months long
after you happened to me like a wrong
number at midnight that blew up the phone
bill to an astronomical unknown
quantity in a foreign currency.
The dollar's dived since you happened to me.
You've grown into your skin since then; you've grown
into the space you measure with someone
you can love back without a caveat.

While I love somebody I learn to live
with through the downpulled winter days' routine
wakings and sleepings, half-and-half caffeine-
assisted mornings, laundry, stock-pots, dust-
balls in the hallway, lists instead of longing, trust
that what comes next comes after what came first.
She'll never be a story I make up.
You were the one I didn't know where to stop.
If I had blamed you, now I could forgive
you, but what made my cold hand, back in prox-

imity to your hair, your mouth, your mind,
want where it no way ought to be, defined
by where it was, and was and was until
the whole globed swelling liquefied and spilled
through one cheek's nap, a syllable, a tear,
was never blame, whatever I wished it were.
You were the weather in my neighborhood.
You were the epic in the episode.
You were the year poised on the equinox.

Chiliastic Sapphics

Sunday afternoon at the end of summer:
from the Place des Vosges come a busking harpist's
liquid notes to lap at the traffic noises
outside my window.

Car horns honk: tail end of a Jewish wedding's
automotive crocodile. Bridal party
at the head, they beep toward the *vingtième*, trailing
limp pink tulle streamers.

Flip in a cassette while I read the papers:
drought and famine, massacres. Cloistered sisters'
voices raise the Kyrie. A gay pastor
who was abducted

last week rated photographs and a headline.
This week, men in uniform: an invasion.
Refugees are interviewed crossing borders,
businessmen taken

hostage. An American in a golf cart
mobilizes teenagers to the oilfields.
Crowds in Jordan volunteer for the jihad's
suicide squadrons.

Tanks and aircraft carriers take position
to wage war for Mecca and petrodollars.
Poison gas is brandished. (The Kurds were gassed, and
then, who protested?)

Death to Jews, to infidels, to invaders!
Kill the Arabs! We're going to blast the bastards
off the planet! Journalists feed the slogans
into computers.

They'll be heard tomorrow in every language
(even taking precedence over football).
Holy war or genocide: peace is everywhere untranslated.

Will she be in love with me when I'm fifty?
Will we still have names and our own diseases?
What's become of Pasteur Doucé? His lover
mourns, while reporters

flock toward war. The nuns who attain their limpid
a cappella *O lumière joyeuse*
made their tape four years ago. They'd be singing
it now, at vespers.

At this moment, six o'clock sunlight blazes
roof and cornice opposite, where the neighbors,
just come home from holidays in the country,
throw open windows,

and the price of nectarines and tomatoes
by the kilo was what competing voices
cried in French and Arabic at the market
early this morning.

Annunciation: 8 A.M.

The plaster-dusted forearms of the boys
scaling the next-door building stretch across
my window. Mallets syncopate their noise
to contrapuntal belches of a bus

downstairs. A huge blue wire-and-plastic tent
covers the scaffolding they clamber up.
Here comes a fifty-pound sack of cement
hooked dubiously to a pulley-rope.

They would have looked like angels to Cocteau:
slick brown arms, backs, chests, flecked with fine white powder.
I turn the dial in search of Radio
Classique. It may require something louder

– Tunisian pop? – to neutralize the racket
of what just looks like self-important Men
At Work to me, too close, who will not pack it
in till noon: their job's the civic one.

My job's the monkish notebook on the pine
table facing the window, white-veiled now.
Beside it lies, light-barred in thin sunshine,
an airmail envelope from someone who

once sat across this table, with the pane
of glass behind the sunburst of her hair
reflecting its flat halo on massed rain
clouds above slate roofs I was glad were there

as an excuse to spend the day indoors.
But that was in another incarnation
whose flesh is paper now, not mine, not hers.
Static crackles the chamber-music station;

drills shatter old façades. The day's begun
officially, that started earlier
with gray light, klaxon of a baker's van,
street-sweepers' slosh, shards of the dream before

I woke splintering into syllables
nobody, after all, is going to say,
between the horn concerto and the drills,
the morning and the rest of the long day.

Quai Saint-Bernard

I take my Sunday exercise riverside,
not quite a local, not quite a transient.
    Dutch houseboats, gravel barges, nose by
    teenagers tanning in day-glo gym shorts.

Waves slick as seal pelts undulate after, like
sun-dappled, ludic, sexual animals
    – if you ignore the floating garbage
    cast by the strollers and weekend sailors.

Three German students nap on their sleeping bags,
backpacks and water bottles niched next to them,
    up on the slope of lawn beside the
    playground, as safe as suburban puppies,

while, underneath a willow, a family:
blonde woman, man like African ebony,
    her mother, almond-golden toddler,
    picnic on Camembert, bread and apples.

I bring my books to sit in my favorite
spot, concrete steps that arc in a half-circle
    out from the water. Sometimes, barges
    pull up and tie up beside my elbow.

Shit! someone's standing inches in back of me,
with all this space … From vision's periphery
    I just can make out it's a woman,
    so I relax. Then she walks around me

on down the quai – a derelict madwoman,
drunk, drugged, or tranced, long hair to her knees, with bare
    feet, flowered blouse and filthy trousers,
    teetering there like a tightrope walker.

She pauses, kneels down, flinging her copious
brown, half-soaked hair, a blindfold, in front of her
    so she can't see where she is going
    inches away from the churning water.

Who stops her, leads her farther away from the
edge, even asks her what she was doing there?
    I don't, although she'd come so close her
    serpentine shadow fell on my notebook.

She halts, and sways in front of a sunbathing
young man engrossed in reading a paperback.
    We others watch her staring at him,
    grateful we aren't the one she's chosen.

No crisis: she traverses the half-circle
stone steps, away from water and audience,
    sits in the dust behind a basalt
    statue, lies down like exhausted dogs do.

So I dismiss her, turn back away from her.
So does the almost-naked man opposite.
    We read, relieved of ever knowing
    even what language she might have spoken.

Letter to Julie in a New Decade

I think of you in all that Irish mist
in which you're writing out your solitude
impatiently: the morning's Eucharist
is gruel, or finnan haddie; clouds intrude
on crag and moor and rain-drenched Gothic heap
– at least, they do when I imagine it.
Up on the hills are huddled flocks of sheep
that leave behind them little cairns of shit.
The men tell whoppers and they drink too much.
They all should do something about their teeth.
Has there been anyone you'd like to touch?
Is there a sunset hike across the heath?
It's going to rain again – the sky's like lead.
Mme. Melhing next door is ninety-nine.
I meet her on the street, her daily bread
tucked in an oilcloth shopping bag (no, mine

is string). At least, the woman the Sécu
sends twice a week said she was ninety-eight
last year. (If you live long enough, you get
a black woman to clean up after you?)
That's only twice a week: five days, she's got
to tend herself. I passed her yesterday
hauling her night-filled plastic chamber pot
to her Turkish-style *WC-sur-palier*.
Across the way, the redhead on the third
floor still chain-smokes shaking out her rugs.
Her mate, in the next window, bends his beard-
ed gray head streetwards while he grooms the dog.
The widow downstairs (I invent that she's
widowed) takes mouthfuls from a red tin cup
she spits out at her ten-foot rubber trees.
A jackhammer was pounding. Now it's stopped
and two black men in orange worker's pants
take five, light up, and lean against their truck.
Like us, I think, they have two continents,
but not, like us, the luxury and luck
to bridge them, while we can. Another friend
told me, on the phone: her lover found
a lump, is having surgery – happened
in days, two lives completely turned around
toward what could be the end of one, of two
together. She's my father's age, and mine.
I thought of him. I also thought of you,
out with your still-young mother, drinking wine,
one month; the next month, you could only cry
at what one, two, oncologists projected.
We're all dying – but she was going to die
at a velocity no one expected.
My father was forty-six years old
before he 'settled down' in a career.
Cancer settled in him. They never told
us what it was. It killed him in a year.
So, *carpe diem*: eat, drink, fuck and write
to glean grace from these chiliastic days?
The left lacks all conviction, and the right –
capitalism with a human face?
If such a beast exists, I haven't met it.
Entrepreneurs and presidents all can
proclaim, then violate the Rights of Man.

As for the rights of woman, oh, forget it.
That's an idea whose day has come, and gone,
they say. Just as an alcoholic tells
herself while tossing back another one:
the 'feminist' is always someone else.
A China-doll-faced Polish lesbian
proclaimed, when you say 'feminists,' *we* see
housewives in aprons, mules and straggly buns
discussing baby crap and recipes.
A Russian poet, equally *mignonne*
but straight, explained that 'feminists,' to her,
meant 'groups of lesbians,' and lesbians
had not formed groups in the USSR.
I heard one on a panel a few nights
ago, read one between two book reviews.
Meanwhile, the Poles rescind abortion rights
and Pamyat opens season on the Jews.
They've got, in Polish, Renée Vivien,
Colette, and *Les Chansons de Bilitis*
– a piquant combination for a *fin*
de siècle in which clitoridectomies
are performed on infants here in France,
posing a quandary for the liberals:
invade the privacy of immigrants
because their custom is to castrate girls?
Sarcasm is too easy when I'm scared
the cocktail party's over, and the feast
of the new century will be prepared
by nationalists, patriarchs and priests.
It's hard to picture fundamentalists
arresting sunbathers and blasting *flics*
while *Blanc Bleu* and *Autour du Monde* persist
in turning bakeries into boutiques
(no *baguettes* in the rue des Francs-Bourgeois,
only *braguettes* on 600-franc jeans)
but jihad followed imam followed shah,
and imams aren't puréed aubergines
(while, in the land that promised that its gold
would be shared work and civil liberties,
big blonde commandoes shoot at twelve-year-olds
and herd them into 'camps' for 'refugees').
But I was going to write to you, not rant
at you (the code word, we both know, is 'shrill'

when some opinionated female won't
address the 'universal' or keep still.)
If I live long enough, my small ambition
is, be the next old lady on the third
floor (blessed with indoor plumbing), in condition
to send the next and next-to-the-last word
to you, in some warm green place, with your grown-up
granddaughter, and dogs, where it's not raining.
I hope we won't be jailed, or veiled, or blown up
and have the energy to keep complaining.

Year's End

for Audre Lorde and Sonny Wainwright

Twice in my quickly disappearing forties
someone called while someone I loved and I were
making love to tell me another woman
had died of cancer.

Seven years apart, and two different lovers:
underneath the numbers, how lives are braided,
how those women's death and lives, lived and died, were
interleaved also.

Does lip touch on lip a memento mori?
Does the blood-thrust nipple against its eager
mate recall, through lust, a breast's transformations
sometimes are lethal?

Now or later, what's the enormous difference?
If one day is good, is a day sufficient?
Is it fear of death with which I'm so eager
to live my life out

now and in its possible permutations
with the one I love? (Only four days later,
she was on a plane headed west across the
Atlantic, work-bound.)

Men and women, mortally wounded where we
love and nourish, dying at thirty, forty,
fifty, not on barricades, but in beds of
unfulfilled promise:

tell me, senators, what you call abnormal?
Each day's obits read as if there's a war on.
Fifty-eight-year-old poet dead of cancer:
warrior woman

laid down with the other warrior women.
Both times when the telephone rang, I answered,
wanting not to, knowing I had to answer,
go from two bodies'

infinite approach to a crest of pleasure
through the disembodied voice from a distance
saying one loved body was clay, one wave of
mind burst and broken.

Each time we went back to each other's hands and
mouths as to a requiem where the chorus
sings death with irrelevant and amazing
bodily music.

Cancer Winter

for Rafael Campo and Hayden Carruth

Syllables shaped around the darkening day's
contours. Next to armchairs, on desks, lamps
were switched on. Tires hissed softly on the damp
tar. In my room, a flute concerto played.
Slate roofs glistened in the rain's thin glaze.
I peered out from a cave like a warm bear.
Hall lights flicked on as someone climbed the stairs
across the street, blinked out: a key, a phrase
turned in a lock, and something flew open.
I watched a young man at his window write
at a plank table, one pooled halogen
light on his book, dim shelves behind him, night
falling fraternal on the flux between
the odd and even numbers of the street.

I woke up, and the surgeon said, 'You're cured.'
Strapped to the gurney, in the cotton gown
and pants I was wearing when they slid me down
onto the table, made new straps secure
while I stared at the hydra-headed O.R.
lamp, I took in the tall, confident, brown-
skinned man, and the ache I couldn't quite call pain
from where my right breast wasn't anymore
to my armpit. A not-yet-talking head,
I bit dry lips. What else could he have said?
And then my love was there in a hospital coat;
then my old love, still young and very scared.
Then I, alone, graphed clock hands' asymptote
to noon, when I would be wheeled back upstairs.

The odd and even numbers of the street
I live on are four thousand miles away
from an Ohio February day
snow-blanketed, roads iced over, with sleet
expected later, where I'm incomplete
as my abbreviated chest. I weigh
less — one breast less — since the Paris-gray
December evening, when a neighbor's feet
coming up ancient stairs, the feet I counted
on paper were the company I craved.
My calm right breast seethed with a grasping tumor.
The certainty of my returns amounted
to nothing. After terror, being brave
became another form of gallows humor.

At noon, an orderly wheeled me upstairs
via an elevator hung with Season's
Greetings streamers, bright and false as treason.
The single room the surgeon let us share
the night before the knife was scrubbed and bare
except for blush-pink roses in a vase on
the dresser. Veering through a morphine haze on
the cranked bed, I was avidly aware
of my own breathing, my thirst, that it was over —
the week that ended on this New Year's Eve.
A known hand held, while I sipped, icewater,
afloat between ache, sleep, lover and lover.
The one who stayed would stay; the one would leave.
The hand that held the cup next was my daughter's.

It's become a form of gallows humor
to reread the elegies I wrote
at that pine table, with their undernote
of cancer as death's leitmotiv, enumer-
ating my dead, the unknown dead, the rumor
of random and pandemic deaths. I thought
I was a witness, a survivor, caught
in a maelstrom and brought forth, who knew more
of pain than some, but learned it loving others.
I need to find another metaphor
while I eat up stories of people's mothers
who had mastectomies. 'She's eighty-four
this year, and *fine!*' Cell-shocked, I brace to do
what I can, an unimportant exiled Jew.

The hand that held the cup next was my daughter's
– who would be holding shirts for me to wear,
sleeve out, for my bum arm. She'd wash my hair
(not falling yet), strew teenager's disorder
in the kitchen, help me out of the bathwater.
A dozen times, she looked at the long scar
studded with staples, where I'd suckled her,
and didn't turn. She took me / I brought her
to the surgeon's office, where she'd hold
my hand, while his sure hand, with its neat tool, snipped
the steel, as on a revised manuscript
radically rewritten since my star
turn nursing her without a 'nursing bra'
from small, firm breasts, a twenty-five-year-old's.

I'm still alive, an unimportant Jew
who lives in exile, voluntarily
or not: Ohio's alien to me.
Death follows me home here, but I pay dues
to stay alive. White cell count under two:
a week's delay in chemotherapy
stretches it out: Ohio till July?
The Nazarenes and Pentecostals who
think drinking wine's a mortal sin would pray
for me to heal, find Jesus, go straight, leave.
But I'm alive, and can believe I'll stay
alive a while. Insomniac with terror,
I tell myself, it isn't the worst horror.
It's not Auschwitz. It's not the Vel d'Hiv.

I had 'breasts like a twenty-five-year-old,'
and that was why, although a mammogram
was done the day of my year-end exam
in which the doctor found the lump, it told
her nothing: small, firm, dense breasts have and hold
their dirty secrets till their secrets damn
them. Out of the operating room
the tumor was delivered, sectioned, cold-
packed, pickled, to demonstrate to residents
an infiltrative ductal carcinoma
(with others of its kind). I've one small, dense
firm breast left, and cell-killer pills so no more
killer cells grow, no eggs drop. To survive
my body stops dreaming it's twenty-five.

It's not Auschwitz. It's not the Vel d'Hiv.
It's not gang rape in Bosnia or
gang rape and gutting in El Salvador.
My self-betraying body needs to grieve
at how hatreds metastasize. Reprieved
(if I am), what am I living for?
Cancer, gratuitous as a massacre,
answers to nothing, tempts me to retrieve
the white-eyed panic in the mortal night,
my father's silent death at forty-eight,
each numbered, shaved, emaciated Jew
I might have been. They wore the blunt tattoo,
a scar, if they survived, oceans away.
Should I tattoo my scar? What would it say?

No body stops dreaming it's twenty-five,
or twelve, or ten, when what is possible's
a long road poplars curtain against loss, able
to swim the river, hike the culvert, drive
through the open portal, find the gold hive
dripping with liquid sweetness. Risible
fantasy, if, all the while, invisible
entropies block the roads, so you arrive
outside a ruin, where trees bald with blight
wane by a river drained to sluggish mud.
The setting sun looks terribly like blood.
The hovering swarm has nothing to forgive.
Your voice petitions the indifferent night:
'I don't know how to die yet. Let me live.'

Should I tattoo my scar? What would it say?
It could say 'K. J.'s Truck Stop' in plain English, highlighted with a nipple ring
(the French version: Chez K. J. / Les Routiers).
I won't be wearing falsies, and one day
I'll bake my chest again at Juan-les-Pins,
round side and flat, gynandre/androgyne,
close by my love's warm flanks (though she's sun-shy
as I should be: it's a carcinogen
like smoked fish, caffeine, butterfat and wine).
O let me have my life and live it too!
She kissed my breasts, and now one breast she kissed
is dead meat, with its pickled blight on view.
She'll kiss the scar, and then the living breast.

I don't know how to die yet. Let me live!
Did Etty Hillesum think that, or Anne Frank,
or the forty-year-old schoolteacher the bank
robber took hostage when the cop guns swiv-
eled on them both, or the seropositive
nurse's aide, who, one long-gone payday, drank
too much, fucked whom? or the bag lady who stank
more than I wished as I came closer to give
my meager change? I say it, bargaining
with the *contras* in my blood, immune
system bombarded but on guard. Who's gone?
The bookseller who died at thirty-nine,
poet, at fifty-eight, friend, fifty-one,
friend, fifty-five. These numbers do not sing.

She'll kiss the scar, and then the living breast,
and then, again, from ribs to pit, the scar,
but only after I've flown back to her
out of the unforgiving Middle West
where my life's strange, and flat disinterest
greets strangers. At Les-Saintes-Maries-de-la-Mer,
lust pulsed between us, pulsed in the plum grove where
figs dropped to us like manna to the blessed.
O blight that ate my breast like worms in fruit,
be banished by the daily pesticide
that I ingest. Let me live to praise
her breathing body in my arms, our wide
branched perennial love, from whose taproot
syllables shape around the lengthening days.

Friends, you died young. These numbers do not sing
your requiems, your elegies, our war
cry: at last, not 'Why me?' but 'No more
one-in-nine, one-in-three, rogue cells killing
women.' You're my companions, traveling
from work to home to the home I left for
work, and the plague, and the poison which might cure.
The late sunlight, the morning rain, will bring
me back to where I started, whole, alone,
with fragrant coffee into which I've poured
steamed milk, book open on the scarred pine table.
I almost forget how close to the bone
my chest's right side is. Unremarkable,
I woke up, still alive. Does that mean 'cured'?

Dusk: July

Late afternoon rain of a postponed summer:
wet streets, wet slate rooves, swish of tires, wet awnings,
pin-curled neighbor leaning out on her wrought-iron
window-guard, smoking,

wet chestnuts, wet lavender by the river's
shades of gray-green. This oversubtle season
will not burst, all clarity, into sunlight.
Petal by petal,

tiger lilies open up in a pitcher,
orange, yellow, stars or beast faces yawning.
Leaves like feast-day offerings round an altar
drop on the carpet.

I would love my love, but my love is elsewhere.
I would take a walk with her in the evening's
milky pearl. I'd sleep with my arms around her
confident body,

arms and legs asprawl like an adolescent.
We're not adolescents. Our friends are dying
and between us nothing at all is settled
except our loving.

We've loved other bodies the years have altered:
knuckles swollen, skin slackened, eyelids grainy;
bodies that have gone back to earth, the synapse
of conscience broken.

Softly, softly, speak of it, but say something.
We are middle-aged and our friends are dying.
What do we lie down beside when we lie down
alone, together?

If I could remember the names, the places,
rooms and faces, gestures and conversations,
I'd have some excuse for the years passed through me
like air, like water:

school friends who turned into suburban matrons;
bar friends, one-night stands, who are dead of AIDS, or
tenured, or in jail, or suburban matrons;
great-aunts, grandparents

of whom I had nothing to tell my daughter.
Those dead Jews on both sides of the Atlantic
disappear again as the year two thousand
washes us under.

Seize the days, the days, or the years will seize them,
leaving just the blink of a burnt-out lightbulb
with a shard of filament left inside that
ticks when it's shaken.

Fix the days in words and the years will seize them
anyway: a bracket of dates, an out-of-
print book, story nobody told, rooms locked and
phone disconnected,

cemetery no one will ever visit.
Who knows where my grandparents' graves are? Who cut
through the gauze unveiling my mother's tombstone?
I don't. I didn't.

Light is still alive in the table lamp I
switch on in the nine o'clock twilight; music
still alive in street noise; mine one more shadow
drawing the curtains.

I just want to wake up beside my love who
wakes beside me. One of us will die sooner;
one of us is going to outlive the other,
but we're alive now.

August Journal

How does it feel, in this ephemeral flesh,
to be back at my work table, to sit
looking out the window while a flush
of late sun brightens scrubbed stone opposite,
illuminates known neighbors' unknown rooms,
just as it shone a year, two years ago
when I, immortal as an eight-year-old,
looked out in my clean, unscarred, unbroken skin
(the oily selfhood I'm sequestered in,
the body I'm not going to leave alive,
whose guard – I didn't know it yet – was down)?
If I'm one of the victims, who survives?
If I'm – reach for it – a survivor, who
are the victims? The heroic dead,
the ones who died in despair, the ones who died
in terror, the exhausted ones who died
tired? I'm tired of terror and despair
and having to be brave. I want the dull
workdays and nights of unexceptional
unmarked life, with eyelashes and hair.
It *is* exceptional to die in bed
at ninety-eight, not having been gassed, shot,
wrung dry with dysentery, drowned at birth
in a basin for unwanted girls.
The unexceptional beg on the street
outside Red Apple, outside Monoprix
(he's young, black, AIDS-thin, with a brindled cat
she's dark-haired, white, butch, with a Labrador),
back in Paris, she's there; back in New York
he's there: if one's gone, when will I know it?
For themselves, they will not disappear:
they'll endure whatever they endure,
two years outside a supermarket door
not being sufficient. Life (and death) hold more
bad cards in store than that, bad cards in store
for the complacent housewives walking by:
the mammogram, the colonoscopy.

The sun seeps in through windows I remember.
Now the young couple on the third-floor-left
have a baby (sometime since December)
and crocheted curtains in the front-room window.
Across the hall from them, the little widow
was away (her rubber tree went sallow,
went brown) but now she's back, and leaning out
to watch the menswear wholesaler's young, stout
Arab apprentice load a truck with suits.
Behind me: silence, an unoccupied
cold-water flat. Madame Mehling has died
at one hundred and two, exceptional
and humdrum as the sparrows that she fed
on fine days, the last night's leftover bread
through two world wars till now. In the damp hall
downstairs, atop the green recycling bin
were piled small, threadbare jackets, dresses, shoes,
aprons, sexagenarian saucepans.
The century of life she had to lose
is lost, the century of memory
evaporated, a scent in the air,
a light, halt step I won't hear on the stairs.
Her fiancé died in the First World War;
she worked four decades in a creamery.
Was it one hundred years of solitude
or of spinsterly sociability
with cronies all around the neighborhood?
Rapid, high-pitched exchanges while TV
noise blared were frequent in the afternoons
as I came up the stairs, thinking that soon
I'd spend an afternoon talking with her.

A century of memory: I talk
as if I could remember: was that walk
along the beach in Normandy before
or after lunch – four days ago! (The war
forty-nine years past, cathedral towers
patched up, museum garden clocked with flowers.)
Carved stones from hen yards, as if magnetized,
pile in the cloister from which they'd been prised
by mercenaries when Napoleon
undid what Jacobins had not undone:
the past – priest-ridden, hunger-blighted, king-

despoiled sump heap where wit, inquiry, reason
flourished for an enigmatic season.
A hundred years before Madame Mehling
was born in some dim suburb, then still green;
a hundred years before my Austrian
Jewish grandparents, both aged sixteen,
fled one more pogrom, as far as London,
the season turned (as it would turn, again):
the flaming summer of a violent spring
promised a raising and a levering,
with Jews and women hailed as 'Citizen.'

And turned again, as it will turn toward fall
where I sit, tethered to a present tense
whose intimations of mortality
may ultimately make no difference
to anyone, except of course to me,
and finally, to nobody at all
(a touch of solipsism worthy of
an acned seventeen-year-old in love).
My life is wider than these windowpanes:
one best-beloved friend, beloved friends
in towns and cities on two continents,
some of whom couldn't pronounce each other's names.
Upon my body is superimposed
the map of a Europe I never knew:
my olive skin, my eyes, my hips, my nose
all mark me as an Ashkenazi Jew
if anyone were looking for a mark
to indicate the designated prey.
I'm more the Jew pursued into the dark
than the scrubbed Yank marching through Normandy.
After our songs became ash on the tongue,
after our tongues were ash, after we took
our leave of being old and being young,
can any Jew stay indoors with a book
and ruminate upon her own disease,
present or past, absorbed, alone, aloof?
I could have been one of the children seized
that day at 22, rue des Ecouffes.
I could have been one of the two-year-olds
not knowing quite how to pronounce my name
penned in a littered courtyard, blotched with cold
behind barbed wire, until the transports came

to what is now a suburb on the way
to the airport, utterly banal,
whose name unflinching bus drivers will say.
Some other names: Touvier, Bousquet, Laval.
I know those names, but not the children's names
'deported to the East' in cattle cars.
Can any Jew praise life and fail to claim
a share for them of bread, of books, of stars?
As if they didn't have enough of stars
and uninflected gray or black or blue
skies glimpsed through grilled gaps from the cattle cars,
stars, skies, they starved and froze and died below.
Later, the patriotic hordes of France
shaved and tarred and whipped the women whose
neighbors said, they slept with the occupants:
not the police who rounded up the Jews;
not the officials who determined 'race';
not the French guards of French internment camps
who hurried their dazed charges up the ramps
into the death trains: passed without a trace
to middle age, old age, to death in bed
(exceptional) perhaps, at ninety-eight,
perhaps having forgotten what they did
without much thought, much mercy, or much hate.
O Europe of old stairways and dead Jews!
But every Saturday at half past noon
black-bearded fathers, pale, dark-suited sons,
daughters in frills and patent-leather shoes
walk home toward lunch from Sabbath services.
(Where are the mothers? They don't have to cook
on Shabbes!) Stubborn people of the Book,
renewed after such disappearances,
though you are not my past, you are my past
(there are no atheists in a pogrom).
My future, though, is coming toward me fast
from elsewhere, and I cannot know where from
– the night-without-a-morning of disease,
the afternoon of long, exceptional
life as summer modulates to fall,
the flame-erupted dusk of history?
All I can know is the expanding moment,
present, infinitesimal, infinite,
in which the late sun enters without comment
eight different sets of windows opposite.

from

SQUARES AND COURTYARDS

(2000)

Scars on Paper

An unwrapped icon, too potent to touch,
she freed my breasts from the camp Empire dress.
Now one of them's the shadow of a breast
with a lost object's half-life, with as much
life as an anecdotal photograph:
me, Kim and Iva, all stripped to the waist,
hiking near Russian River on June first
'79: Iva's five-and-a-half.
While *she* was almost twenty, wearing black
T-shirts in D.C., where we hadn't met.
You lay your palm, my love, on my flat chest.
In lines alive with what is not regret,
she takes her own path past, doesn't turn back.
Persistently, on paper, we exist.

Persistently, on paper, we exist.
You'd touch me if you could, but you're, in fact,
three thousand miles away. And my intact
body is eighteen months paper: the past
a fragile eighteen months regime of trust
in slash-and-burn, in vitamin pills, backed
by no statistics. Each day I enact
survivor's rituals, blessing the crust
I tear from the warm loaf, blessing the hours
in which I didn't or in which I did
consider my own death. I am not yet
statistically a survivor (that
is sixty months.) On paper, someone flowers
and flares alive. I knew her. But she's dead.

She flares alive. I knew her. But she's dead.
I flirted with her, might have been her friend,
but transatlantic schedules intervened.
She wrote a book about her Freedom Ride,
the wary elders whom she taught to read,
– herself half-British, twenty-six, white-blonde,
with thirty years to live.
                    And I happened
to open up *The Nation* to that bad
news which I otherwise might not have known

(not breast cancer: cancer of the brain).
Words take the absent friend away again.
Alone, I think, she called, alone, upon
her courage, tried in ways she'd not have wished
by pain and fear: her courage, extinguished.

The pain and fear some courage extinguished
at disaster's denouement come back
daily, banal: is that brownish-black
mole the next chapter? Was the ache enmeshed
between my chest and armpit when I washed
rogue cells' new claw, or just a muscle-ache?
I'm not yet desperate enough to take
comfort in being predeceased: the anguish
when the Harlem doctor, the Jewish dancer,
die of AIDS, the Boston seminary's
dean succumbs 'after brief illness' to cancer.
I like mossed slabs in country cemeteries
with wide-paced dates, candles in jars, whose tallow
glows on summer evenings, desk-lamp yellow.

Aglow in summer evening, a desk-lamp's yellow
moonlight peruses notebooks, houseplants, texts,
while an aging woman thinks of sex
in the present tense. Desire may follow,
urgent or elegant, cut raw or mellow
with wine and ripe black figs: a proof, the next
course, a simple question, the complex
response, a burning sweetness she will swallow.
The opening mind is sexual and ready
to embrace, incarnate in its prime.
Rippling concentrically from summer's gold
disc, desire's iris expands, steady
with blood-beat. Each time implies the next time.
The aging woman hopes she will grow old.

The aging woman hopes she will grow old.
A younger woman has a dazzling vision
of bleeding wrists, her own, the clean incisions
suddenly there, two open mouths. They told
their speechless secrets, witnesses not called
to what occurred with as little volition
of hers as these phantom wounds.
                                        Intense precision
of scars, in flesh, in spirit. I'm enrolled
by mine in ranks where now I'm 'being brave'
if I take off my shirt in a hot crowd
sunbathing, or demonstrating for Dyke Pride.
Her bravery counters the kitchen knives'
insinuation that the scars be made.
With, or despite our scars, we stay alive.

'With, or despite our scars, we stayed alive
until the Contras or the government
or rebel troops came, until we were sent
to "relocation camps," until the archives
burned, until we dug the ditch, the grave
beside the aspen grove where adolescent
boys used to cut class, until we went
to the precinct house, eager to behave
like citizens...'
                        I count my hours and days,
finger for luck the word-scarred table which
is not my witness, shares all innocent
objects' silence: a tin plate, a basement
door, a spade, barbed wire, a ring of keys,
an unwrapped icon, too potent to touch.

Days of 1994: Alexandrians

for Edmund White

Lunch: as we close the twentieth century,
death, like a hanger-on or a wannabe
   sits with us at the cluttered bistro
   table, inflecting the conversation.

Elderly friends take lovers, rent studios,
plan trips to unpronounceable provinces.
   Fifty makes the ironic wager
   that his biographer will outlive him –

as may the erudite eighty-one-year-old
dandy with whom a squabble is simmering.
   His green-eyed architect companion
   died in the spring. He is frank about his

grief, as he savors spiced pumpkin soup, and a
sliced rare filet. We'll see the next decade in
   or not. This one retains its flavor.
   'Her new book…' '…brilliant!' 'She slept with…' '*Really!*'

Long arabesques of silver-tipped sentences
drift on the current of our two languages
   into the mist of late September
   mid-afternoon, where the dusk is curling

★

Just thirty-eight: her last chemotherapy
treatment's the same day classes begin again.
   I went through it a year before she
   started; but hers was both breasts, and lymph nodes.

She's always been a lax vegetarian.
Now she has cut out butter and cheese, and she
   never drank wine or beer. What else is
   there to eliminate? Tea and coffee…

(Our avocado salads are copious.)
It's easier to talk about politics
    than to allow the terror that shares
    both of our bedrooms to find words. It made

the introduction; it's an acquaintance we've
in common. Trading medical anecdotes
    helps out when conversation lapses.
    We don't discuss Mitterrand and cancer.

Four months (I say) I'll see her, see him again.
(I dream my life; I wake to contingencies.)
    Now I walk home along the river,
    into the wind, as the clouds break open.

Squares and Courtyards

Across the Place du Marché Ste-Catherine
the light which frames a building that I see
daily, walking home from the bakery,
white voile in open windows, sudden green
and scarlet window-box geraniums
backlit in cloud-encouraged clarity
against the century-patinaed gray
is such a gift of the quotidian,
a benefice of sight and consciousness,
I sometimes stop, confused with gratitude,
not knowing what to thank or whom to bless,
break off an end of seven-grain baguette
as if my orchestrated senses could
confirm the day. It's fragrant. I eat it.

Confirm the day's fragrance. I eat, bit
by bit, the buttery *pain aux raisins*
shell-coiled beside my steaming afternoon
tea. It's the hour for a schoolchild's treat,
munched down, warm in waxed paper, on the street,
or picked at on chipped earthenware (like mine)
beside books marked with homework to be done
while the street's sunlit, dusk-lit, lamplit.
She sucks her pencil, window-framed. I sip
nostalgia for a childhood not my own
Bronx kitchen table, with a fire-escape
in the alley shaded by sumac trees
which filtered out the other languages
I heard the airshaft's cross-currents intone.

I heard the airshaft's cross-currents intone
below the minyan davening morning offices.
A childish rasp that slurred and sputtered was
the Polish janitor's red-knuckled son
helping his father empty garbage cans.
His voice was why I thought him rough (as is
English when spoken by its novices)
a voice I never heard speaking its own
language. His name was Joseph. He was six.
Other syllables connected news
from gutted Europe to the dusty motes
of Sabbath morning. Ash settled on bricks,
spun up the shaft with voices of old Jews,
was drawn down garrulous chain-smokers' throats.

Drawn up from garrulous chain-smokers' throats
at round tin tables on wet cobblestones
just hosed down by a green-clad African
street-cleaner: strikes, prices, who still votes
Left, sex, a sick child. Hands unbutton coats
halfway. The wind's mild, but it looks like rain
above the Place du Marché Ste-Catherine
where charcoal-bellied clouds converge like boats
in the mutable blue harbor sky.
Another coffee, another *blanc sec* –
as if events were ours to rearrange
with words, as if dailiness forestalled change,
as if we didn't grow old (or not) and die
as long as someone listened when we spoke.

As long as someone listened when I spoke,
especially someone walking a dog,
I'd launch into juvenile monologue:
Greek myths, canine behavior – and could I stroke
the Lab or spaniel? Speech and touch invoked
my grandmother, the bookkeeper from Prague,
who died as I emerged out of the fog
of infancy, while lives dispersed in smoke
above the camps (and Dresden, and Japan)
and with them, someone else I might have been
if memory braided with history.
I pressed my face into the dog's warm fur
whose heat and smell I learned by heart, while she
receded into words I found for her.

Receding into words I found for her
delight, someone was dispossessed of her own
story (she thought) by mine.
                                    Receding in-
to words, the frail and early-rising neighbor
who died during my cancer-treatment year
is not summed up by 'centenarian.'
Her century requires a lexicon.
I wrote a girl on paper when I bore
a child, whose photocopied life became
letters tattooed across a watermark,
a woman's in the world, who shares her name.
And Gísela, who took me to the park,
for whom I pieced together sentences
– it's all the words she said to me I miss.

It's all the words she said to me I miss,
down to unechoed accents. Did she speak
Yiddish to me? With whom did she speak Czech?
German was what my father spoke till his
sixth year, first grade (when did he tell me this?)
– his parents' common tongue. And did they make
love in their second language? The air's thick
with cognates, questions and parentheses
she'll scribble down once she's back in her room,
chewing her braid, tracing our labyrinthine
fragments. She zips her anorak
and shifts the heavy satchel on her back

watching low clouds gather as she walks home
across the Place du Marché Ste-Catherine.

Not knowing what to thank or whom to bless,
the schoolgirl at the window, whom I'm not,
hums cadences it soothes her to repeat
which open into other languages
in which she'll piece together sentences
while I imagine her across the street
as late light shifts, sunlit, dusk-lit, lamplit.
Is there a yellow star sewed to her dress
as she exults, confused with gratitude,
her century requires a lexicon
of memory braided with history
she'll have reflective decades to write down?
Not thinking, she'll get old (or not) and die;
thinking: she can, if anybody could.

Rue Debelleyme

Rain from the channel: wind and rain again
umbrellas jostle on the pavement, crowd
together, move apart. Atlantic rain

south from the British Isles. A monocloud
covers the sky that yesterday was blue
and filled with light, where clement winds allowed

expansive breathing, new air flowing through
a sentence or a ribbon or a song
children sang complicated verses to:

a day I could be grateful to for long
light: although not June, still just July
when no direction was entirely wrong

for finding points to take my bearings by
and walk around the corner of a street
that's always there, a small discovery.

If you've misplaced the key, the door is shut
but every street's a door that opens up,
the narrow gangway to a bannered boat:

run up before it raises anchor, slip-
ping otter-like from moorings. On the dock
hands wave bright scarves, and colored pennants flap.

A bus pulled out, a taxi stopped, a truck
parked curbside, the driver undid a latch,
put down a ramp, rolled out a garment-rack.

Two black girls on boot-skates stopped to watch,
dusty from play, homebound at one o'clock
with nectarines and two baguettes for lunch.

(If you've misplaced the key, you're out of luck,
but every window framed another key
A garden past the crossing winked back black,

copper, gold children to their serious play.)
Sisters, from their matching innocent
navy-blue pleats hemmed short above the knee.

(Somewhere in the next *arrondissement*
women do piecework in small factories,
mostly undocumented immigrants,

Filipina, African, Chinese,
some of whose children become secular
and republican *lycéens*.) Did these

two with neat ribbons in their cornrowed hair
and roller-skating scabs on their bare knees
memorize La Fontaine and Baudelaire,

and did the rack of one cloned summer dress
with lime-green polka dots and large puffed sleeves
remind them of the end-of-term *kermesse*,

the job their mother hardly ever leaves,
or some preadolescent feminine
world I wouldn't recognize, believe,

or, with the best-intentioned will, imagine?
Their futures opening like a painted fan:
hairdresser, film director, *lycéenne*,

they skated off, one with the nectarines
the other with the loaves under her arm
towards a deserved repast of citizens,

(as I imagined going home with them
the driver, padlocking his empty van,
set off an inadvertent car-alarm)

the lost key in some jacket pocket found
as, equally irrelevant, the rain
clouds open out onto the blue of noon.

from *Paragraphs from a Day-Book*

for Hayden Carruth

Thought thrusts up, homely as a hyacinth
wrapped in its bulb like a root-vegetable,
a ninth-month
belly, while the green indelible
pattern's inscribed into the labyrinth.
Lanced into light, it's air's inhabitant
with light and air as food and drink.
A hyacinth, tumescent pink
on the low wooden Mexican chest
confronts the wintry dusk
with informed self-interest.
Leaf-spears extravagantly ask
what idea, still gnarled up in a knot
of ganglions, will break through the husk
shaped at last, recognizable as thought

★

Trace, on a city map, trajectories
of partially forgotten words
along the river's arteries,
volatile substance of a sentient world.
Mauve heather crowds the window-grill. The light
lingers a little later, with a slight
vernal inflection. In a moon-glazed vase
bloom yellow freesias, like some rainy day's
brook-bank, in someone else's memory.
Small whirlpools of perception widen, ring
an infant's numinous discoveries
of syllables for animals, toys, trees:
a Lab's thick coat, the dusty birds
in Claremont Park each tardy urban spring,
a stuffed pink leather horse with button eyes.

★

A question-mark in yellow overalls,
I could read. I was three.
I slept with that pink horse. My one doll's
name was V.J. She'd been given to me
to celebrate the Victory
over Japan, that is to say, the Bomb
I'd spend my schooldays taking shelter from.
I couldn't tie my shoes. But Reddy the fox,
Tootle the engine who jumped off the tracks,
spelled me their stories on my mother's lap
despite weak eyes and poor small-motor skills.
My grandparents were dead: not in pogroms,
not in the camps – of strokes and heart attacks,
merely immigrants, not deportees.
'When you die, does everything just stop?'

★

Grief, pain and sorrow all are '*la douleur*,'
while '*le bonheur*' is simple happiness
which we savored in the hour
seized as the solstice passed
across the heather-misted calendar
whose olive-brown hillocks' December blur
was pierced by the setting sun
as we meandered, *vigneron*
to *vigneron*, well-spring to orchard, stopped
for *Le Monde*, for the view,
pleasure both cumulative and abrupt:
sudden suave vista; beauty we knew
(mist imperceptibly becoming rain)
well enough to recall, while going through
the nuances of sorrow, grief and pain.

★

My life ago, in this renascent slum
shabby Jews in sweatshops, with irregular
papers, wherever they came from,
gathered mid-morning around a samovar
enthroned amidst rows of Singer sewing-machines.
They trusted the Republic. They were last seen
being beaten with rifle-butts onto sealed trains.
Their great-nephews are Orthodox extremists;
their great-nieces are hash-smoking anarchists.
Some of the sweatshops are high-priced oak-beamed flats,
but I live in one of their tenements
with smeared hallways, corroded pipes, centenarian drains
and five flights of ancient, patinaed spiral stairs,
getting junk mail from clothes-jobbers and bureaucrats,
sheltered from fascists and the elements.

★

When I've described my life like this, I've lied.
I also live in six airy rooms on upper Broadway
just south of Harlem, which I bought when my mother died
– a school-teacher whose penury
left me the wherewithal for bedroom windows
with a view, two long blocks west, of the Hudson.
One friend thinks I'm a coddled American
hypocrite after she spent ten days with me there:
America, whose deep thumbprint of blood's on
cachectic brows from the Bronx to Zaire.
Addicts with AIDS warehoused in SROs
hidden on side-streets south of Riverside
Drive might not find Sarajevo
or Kigali on a map, but tonight, they know
people like them will starve and freeze somewhere

★

– which is Saturday night, so that's where my lover
is giving out condoms and clean syringes
door to door, floor to floor. Someone's had fever
for a week. She's shown an abcessed sore. Nobody scrounges
quarters or cigarettes.
                Some rooms are neat.
Their tenants ask her in. There's a hot-plate,
a kettle, pictures of cats from a magazine
taped to the wall. She sits on the chenille
bedspread, and hears about the son, fourteen,
who lives with his grandmother outside Asheville.
There are some rooms she'd rather not go in.
                    Her
colleagues, two medical students and a nurse,
each with a backpack and a sharps container
come down the stairs from the upper floors.
                    Of course
she knocks on those doors, and goes in, when she's asked in.

★

At nine or so, she's done, and there's a table
set, amber liquid threading ice,
a cork drawn, bread broken, companionable
alto spirals, pulsed by the bass;
on the street, slang and sirens of upper Manhattan.
Robert is dead, and Melissa, and Geraldine,
Larry, Angel. Doris started Crixivan.
So did Wilhelmina. They're both in wheelchairs.
The grainy blow-up on a gallery
wall — a man slumped onto a leatherette
sofa, eyes open, pupils rolled back: dead
is snapshot legacy or prophecy.
The smart-ass golden boy photographer,
Kevin, who started the needle exchange from his van
died in his living room of an overdose.

SOME TRANSLATIONS
1998–2004

SOME TRANSLATIONS
1950–2004

from *A Long Gone Sun* (2000)
by Claire Malroux

'In violet circles'

In violet circles
the school bell
calls us back at dusk
from the allotment garden
my father plants and tends not far from the village
Identical others unroll
their vegetable beds
on ground flat as a swamp
There, children play forbidden games
exploring their uncertain borders
in huts of wild reeds
Coming from who knows where
bats begin
their zigzagging flight
Proud garlic blooms hoist themselves on spindly stems
violet tears at the edge of their lashes
as if the bell had drunk their color
before calling us into the shadows

'Cricket hunts are also in the evening'

Cricket hunts are also in the evening
when the first stars
emerge from their den
our buttocks down on the teeming earth
(for to capture a cricket
you have to deluge its hole with urine
then the insect dislodged by the hot flood
will teeter on the edge of its shelter)
noses in the weeds
or eyes lifted toward the sky's protecting headdress
whose edges grew lighter
like the gray temples of an ancestor
It's a very peaceable hunt
mostly spent waiting
We don't speak, scattered in the field
instead, we live moments of prayer

listening to the dark worship
tapped by the night from earth's entrails
Pathetic in the Grass
A minor nation celebrates
Its unobtrusive Mass
Perhaps the last sound to be silenced
when the planet gives up the ghost
for, in case of apocalypse
we imagine that birds
would choose suicide
throwing themselves all at once against the sky

'It was a long week of delights beginning'

It was a long week of delights beginning
Alain-Fournier writes of Christmas
when, to see him, his fictitious grandparents had
crossed the whole province
(his real grandfather was born in my home town)
loaded down with packets of chestnuts, with delicacies
wrapped up in cloth napkins
My widowed grandfather arrives alone and empty-handed
He wears the black of the mine which ground down his life
the sorrow of his wind-whipped house
my father's cradle
deep in a narrow hollow stripped of greenery
the mouldy smell of his retirement, stretched
between the clock's large eye
and the gaudy diamonds of the bedside rug
clashing their colors
He lives in one room: the back of his house
is rented out to Poles
and the room beyond the scullery
is reserved for our rare visits

★

Two beds, the photos of the couple hung on the walls
our involuntary jailers: two beings
whose eyes don't meet
My pious grandmother
has no voice but her wide mosaic eyes

and the wind's lament
to convince her secular spouse
and their unbelieving descendants
of her soul's eternal life.

★

My grandfather comes to visit us but goes right back out
I find him again later at the constable's
to whom I bring the newspaper
at the hour when roaming dogs bark
scenting corridors of anguish in narrow back streets
He's enthroned among his listeners
He brings them news of an incredible country
where a man need only stoop to gather diamonds
instead of digging them by the sweat of his brow
Perhaps he tells them that he saw Jaurès
with his own eyes, touched him with his own hands
and that he heard Jaurès say one day we'd share
all the diamonds in the world.

'Beauty comes from Spain'

Beauty comes from Spain
exiled by civil war
For her concert appearances she wears
ethereal white tulle dresses
over whose necklines
her ringlets unfurl in a blonde waterfall
Beauty speaks another language
so she has no conversation with the one
who accompanies her across the town square
with its endless comings and goings
The little escort voluptuously bathes
in the admiration flowing toward her companion
Who, she asks herself, could resist the fairy-tale hair
and infinitely clear eyes of the Catalan
that muff hiding the precious hands
which she has seen placed, at her parents' bidding
on the keys of her own piano
under the tall bronze vases
made of bomb-casings from the Great War

True love is like this, perhaps
absolute self-forgetfulness
in fact she has melted into Beauty's shadow
until she feels only a point of ecstatic pain
like the injection before anesthesia
and losing consciousness
Years later she happens to look at a photograph
signed affectionately to her family
which had sheltered the young woman in those troubled times
Under the ringlets between the rounded forehead
and the flounced sleeves
she detects in the delicate features
a hint of Latin heaviness
apparent also in the slightly too-plump arms
She wonders if that hair was really blond
She muses that love is all the more extreme
because it's duped by appearances
but without appearances
there'd be no love

★

On another photograph from those same years
Largo Caballero's striped shirt
pulled tight across his belly
sleeves rolled up and collar open
faces my father's polka-dot bow-tie
which looks like a double-six of dominoes
The dice were thrown without their knowing it
They stand in front of the decrepit wall
of the railway-crossing guard's old cottage
which served as the provisional refuge of the president
of the provisional government of Republican Spain
The two men are steeped waist-high in shadow
which gives their eyes
a look at once inspired and blind
like Borges'

from *Here There Was Once a Country* (2001)
by *Vénus Khoury-Ghata*

from *The Seven Honeysuckle Sprigs of Wisdom*

My village has three waterfalls three churches but no priest
The last one went off after a crow that cawed in Aramaic

Time in my village is in such a hurry that women whelp litters in
seven days no skimpier than the ones you'd see elsewhere

My village's river turns back toward its source to avoid flowing
through the neighboring hamlet with its wealth of three cars and
an embalmed saint which attracts pilgrims

★

In my village the sheep are so tall they graze on clouds' bellies,
chew in the violets' shadows while slandering Mansour the
wool-carder

In the beginning was the egg repeats Rahil morning and night and
she breaks her rooster's eggs on the ironsmith's anvil
Rahil who was a communist well before Lenin and Siberia won't
judge anyone since her son slept with her she-goat and then
bought her three necklaces and a gold nose-ring

Sometimes silhouettes loom up on the highest hilltop
ibex or wolf it makes no difference
Rahil's ball of yarn dissolves and knits coats for anyone who's cold

★

Roads which cross other people's dreams lead nowhere
says Massouda the wise woman while blowing into the stem of her
narguileh
Her smoke-rings make the canary dizzy; he suspects the earth of
speeding up its rotation to reach night more quickly, night
which fades his mistress' beauty

Massouda's cards never lie
Three aces followed by three jacks mean a plague of locusts
A change of mayor is inevitable when three kings line up on the table
Massouda's counsels are listened to by the archbishop whose Mass
    she prompts by making her bench creak

Khalid who made a fortune selling oats buttons up his fly on his
    marble balcony within sight of his mare
She recognizes him by the odor of his sweat and by his whip
    which lashes the clouds during droughts to make them rain on
    his field

★

This selfsame Khalid had his head plunged in a basin of water
    perfumed with orange-blossoms when the bombing made his
    house crash to the ground
He regained his balance on a flagstone without spilling a drop of water

Maroun has quit his job in the brickyard to set up shop as a liar
He lies in winter especially when the wind busy howling in the
    gullies can't contradict him
Maroun claims to have downed a dozen quail with a stone
and to have started a storm by pissing in the wind
He surprised everyone by taking off for America with his coffee-pot
leaving his wife on the kitchen wall, hanging from a nail

The beggar Rassoul's mouth waters till it drips at the sight of Laouza
her belly is a white loaf blessed by the archbishop
her navel a cherry pecked by blackbirds

★

The priest the rabbi and the imam invited to the poor man's table,
brought him three tufts of their beards which he planted in his garden
The three upside-down trees which grew nine months later
cast their shade on the devil's house

The schoolmaster Farhoud is so conscientious that he tries the
    alphabet out on himself before using it on the children
The letter Aleph is unreliable
its back is so fragile not even a hair could ride on it
'Mim' is an ardent she-camel listening to the muezzin

'Ba' prefers jam to the dictionary
'Sin' is a coffee-pot with a pierced ear
'Zah's' axles creak since 'tah' crushed its toe
'Tah' can only be learned lying down standing up is bad for him

Farhoud lived in geography for a long time before moving into
   grammar
Asia Minor he says is only Asia Major's younger sister
and the poles an invention of a bear with a bad idea

Six Poems by Hédi Kaddour

The Bus Driver

What has gotten into the bus driver
Who has left his bus, who has sat down
On a curb on the Place de l'Opéra
Where he slips into the ease of being
Nothing more than his own tears? The passers-by
Who bend over such a shared and
Presentable sorrow would like him
To tell them that the wind used to know
How to come out of the woods towards a woman's dress,
Or that one day his brother said to him
Even your shadow wants nothing to do with you.
His feet in a puddle, the bus driver
Can only repeat *This work is hard*
And people aren't kind.

The Scarab Bookshop

It might be on the front steps of a dream,
Her pink skirt, the ribbon in her hair
At sixty. 'Can you spare me a tenner?'
She insists, as you stare
At your own childhood in those old books
Babar's Journey, Mitchi
The Bearcub, motherless in the window
While, behind your back, all of your old
Loves have returned to lurk around
The foot of the Montagne Ste-Geneviève.
A time when you have let yourself slip
On your own shadow, while on memory's
Ebb-tide there rises in sublime
Odiferousness, a belch of cheap booze.

Spiritual Distress

And damn the almanac-makers who leave you
stuck between debts and death
or a week with seven tomorrows. Today
here's another gent: *History's convulsions,*
monstrous metaphor of our
spiritual distress. Listen to this, distress:
in Burgos, in the Middle Ages, a baker's son
converted to Christianity, and his father
in a fury, flung him into the oven.
Saint Mary, says the chronicle, saved the son and
the citizens of Burgos burned the father and

don't wander too far off, distress, and start to giggle
because what comes next is a riddle: my first is
a convoy of Jews sent to Auschwitz by
the Préfecture of the Gironde; my second, a procession
of bullet-bloated Algerians who float
under the Pont Mirabeau; my third the funding
of a national political party in the sixties,
and together they make the *proper name* of a great
spiritual distress which is certainly not called
Martin Heidegger and don't get annoyed, what's annoying
is that all this should merely be allusion.

Rue de Tournon

Joseph Roth

A young girl once came to see him; in her hand
Was a straw hat reminiscent of
Crickets and poppies; then
War destroyed the ancient Empire
Where justice occasionally renounced
Its dragon's teeth. Later on
Shadows of the chimneys, cry after cry,
Caught up with life, which fled
Here to the street named for a cardinal
While alcohol seeped through his own
Irony. Examining his plaque, memory
Searches for those bursts of light which he
Could nonetheless draw from the play
Of light and shadow on cities' stone.

Six-Thirty

The Inspector General of Mines
Follows a badly-played
Tennis-match with his eyes. He died
In eighteen-eighty-two
But only after having organized
A World's Fair. At the foot of the statue
An adolescent in a summer dress
Has seated herself astride
Her boyfriend's thighs
And pretends to rape
Him. In the late afternoon air
Come to cool them with an orchard's odor
And echoed words on joblessness and labor,
The boy resists, emitting little cries.

Variations

She already knows that he had said 'The rest of them
shit marble' and that he sometimes played
in, shall we say, disorderly houses (it's
in *Amadeus*), which produced, *Ah, vous dirais-je*,
a taste with the notes' sweetness, between marches
and flourishes, where time gives nothing away,
she plays, re mi do *tou-our-ment*, a mi
that's a quarter-note in a big word,
to utter the right misstep, and silence
is not a figure walking away: it's there to
bring everything together when it's crossed
by fiery certainties, the other hand's arpeggios. Later
the heart's wheeling, drunkenness, shattered words,
or holding on to stars. Tonight *Ah, vous dirais-je*
is only the start of the race, and already
the ironic reflection of herself, while utopia
stays discreetly behind the lamp in
mama's hands, tonight, time is an octave.

Four Seasons for Jude Stéfan
by Guy Goffette

Autumn

Life useless under the scribble of names
it's ourselves already beneath the banner of deceased
futures, ourselves again in the bitter smell
of yellow leaves that the sea

is condensing in this hazy distance, ourselves
who dream of leaving, despondent birds
on the cord of emptiness connecting
the night of bedrooms to the one of desire,

which breaks all at once, at the window
of waking, the stubborn body of the earth
seized by frost. O chrysanthemums, give back
to our sobered bodies a bit of the color

of women who pass by laughing.

Winter

I

The nursing home leans on the boarding-school and already
each of us marks his place as a starving
ancient through the gaps in the hedge, tawny
eye striped with gray blades (O cypress)

– and with tears soon enough when the bus
will have passed, when, the cell closed up
like a fist on the floor-wax and the male
odor, death will lie down

naked among us, marking
a place as well, o jealous of bodies
which so lit up, so (and so swiftly
fizzled out) at the storm-stockinged legs

of fifteen-year-old Suzannes.

II

Everything staked, mad love, on water which weeps
on the pane in December, with no retinue
of white-robed monks (but not without exhilaration),
everything staked, on the waning of tall proud trees

haloed with childhood where for hours
we would stand vigil over the flat villages like
heaped plates in the green tides of valleys:
they lie in our depths now

like the sea, and who will raise them, who
if love is nothing but a wild wave
falling, when we would have wished it
like a ploughshare in the earth of exhausted forgetfulness,

a ploughshare uprooting the chaff of the future.

Spring

I

To begin again, to be reborn, that's
what the Master really said, which we
did not understand. We would look at
the earth's belly, at the clouds, the sky

and remain blind, while the swallow
returned to the selfsame place, resumed
possession of the wind. And we, who would have so
preferred to depart, we stay on the threshold

not knowing where to go, like prisoners
of an invisible map, and of the fear of losing,
while diving into the April light,
the taste of water, the perfume of shadows

and the pleasure of always putting off till tomorrow.

II

But tomorrow is a word with no future
on the wind's scale. Look at your dog
languorous on the grass: she is going to die
and in her shadowed eyes the motionless

light trembles, a caress of the passing
present. Time for her is an empty
house, which floats in the cat's bowl.
Open the door: she applauds

with her whole misshapen ugly body.
All she waits for is your shadow,
owning nothing, except that image of you
which swells space in an instant

and sets the earth in motion at your call.

Summer

Devour, fire, lovely fire with she-demons' tongues
all these papers, these books, these dead letters
and the old man full of rancor and full
of night, devour him

with the bad play of his life, that old
score for one hand on the heart's stage
while the other one saws the air in the wings
seeking what? a love

which doesn't lock the shutters
of the horizon, but bears its flames
up above us in the spreading dusk: love
which resembles you, fire

but like a stone in the palm of noon.

Three Poems by Emmanuel Moses

Royal Blue

Something unknown melts beneath our footsteps
the nights have left us nothing
photographs of what occurred are still discussed
but the history which prevails,
is that of churches' white roses

★

Crush the fires of Prussia beneath a dark heel
every façade bleeds
bleeding, the trees strip themselves
the people are a flock of steaming pigs
on the way to the sty

★

There shall be no other center but the snow
cut short my breath O greatest light
covering the oaks beneath the old city walls
words doze in the wide sensual bed
where even green sap dares not wake them

Old Conversations

He had remembered old conversations with this one and that one
Viaticums which seemed to him to be past use,
In a room almost entirely occupied by a baby grand piano
While in the middle of the square a streetlight crackled,
A little square, German and western, in the shade of a pine,
But especially on the bench at Greenwich,
The sky immense, dusk falling
On the line of poplars bordering the lawn
Where children played football, people walked their dogs,
And a few old men strolled before returning to the close air
And medicinal odor of their rooms,
A twin-engined plane descended towards a neighboring club,
Mim had told him one had to be able to talk about oneself
Or one would end up talking about nothing else,
The former breaker of hearts from Moscow to Czernowitz,
The guitarist with chestnut curls and a childish pout,
At present a little man approaching fifty,
Stooped, with an émigré's timid smile,
With his cabled sweater, his bargain boots,
The bitter fatalism of someone who's known hope,
Has seen it grow and fly away
Leaving him alone with his risky, if not pitiful present,
The two-room apartment in a working-class suburb, the pursuit of
    fees,
The candle-end economies,
The son who stayed in the old country, the daughter who left,
The wife hardened by betrayal and neglect,
Showing by every word and gesture
That it is too late to start over,
Who contents herself with drifting without resistance
And with an infinite patience
For what has she to expect that she hasn't already lost,
Even Grad, pacing the apartment from end to end,
Probably already invaded by metastases,

Had shown reticence,
One does not try to escape the Almighty's will with impunity,
Even in embarking for far-away places,
By stretching out on the partition and giving in to sleep,
He had gotten his fingers burnt –
No one else here, between the Hôpital St.-Louis and the Institut
   Curie
Had had the guts to do it –
And no one would be saved without embarking on the same road,
Bitter, hard.

Café Lirico

Majorca, 2004

Farewell to your villages of rose-scented soap
my lyric island
to your lemon trees ogling naked women
at poolside
like the elders in Scripture
farewell horses with bandaged pasterns
black pigs sleeping side by side with turkeys
farewell silky, laughing sky
escaped from the mountains' too-brief embrace
farewell thistles farewell poppies
farewell dry stone walls of long-past days
battleships and birds stay in dock
last defenders of the Christian palaces
still haunted by innumerable Sicilian shadows
the call to prayer is stilled the baths are no longer steaming
but the bell-tower still looks towards an incongruous east
with the royal verdigris-tinted angel
in the off-hours the Phoenician and the Greek
exchange gossip in their shop doorways
they tire their eyes searching the horizon beyond the ramparts
neither Rome nor Belisarius will return
farewell to the gems of the bishop's palace
the two silver pomegranates looted from some synagogue
no doubt since transformed into a church or convent
farewell my lyrical cafés

from

DESESPERANTO

(2003)

Crepuscule with Muriel

Instead of a cup of tea, instead of a milk-
silk whelk of a cup, of a cup of nearly six-
o'clock teatime, cup of a stumbling block,
cup of an afternoon unredeemed by talk,
cup of a cut brown loaf, of a slice, a lack
of butter, blueberry jam that's almost black,
instead of tannin seeping into the cracks
of a pot, the void of an hour seeps out, infects
the slit of a cut I haven't the wit to fix
with a surgeon's needle threaded with fine-gauge silk
as a key would thread the cylinder of a lock.
But no key threads the cylinder of the lock.
Late afternoon light, transitory, licks
the place of the absent cup with its rough tongue, flicks
itself out beneath the wheel's revolving spoke.
Taut thought's gone, with a blink of attention, slack,
a vision of 'death and distance in the mix'
(she lost her words and how did she get them back
when the corridor of a day was a lurching deck?
The dream-life logic encodes in nervous tics
she translated to a syntax which connects
intense and unfashionable politics
with morning coffee, Hudson sunsets, sex;
then the short-circuit of the final stroke,
the end toward which all lines looped out, then broke.)
What a gaze out the window interjects:
on the south-east corner, a black Lab balks
tugged as the light clicks green toward a late-day walk
by a plump brown girl in a purple anorak.
The Bronx-bound local comes rumbling up the tracks
out of the tunnel, over west Harlem blocks
whose windows gleam on the animal warmth of bricks
rouged by the fluvial light of six o'clock.

Ghazal on Half a Line by Adrienne Rich

In a familiar town, she waits for certain letters,
working out the confusion and the hurt in letters.

Whatever you didn't get – the job, the girl –
rejections are inevitably curt in letters.

This is a country with a post office
where one can still make oneself heard in letters.

(Her one-street-over neighbor's Mme. de Sévigné
who almost always had the last word in letters.)

Was the disaster pendant from a tongue
one she might have been able to avert in letters?

Still, acrimony, envy, lust, disdain
are landmines the unconscious can insert in letters.

Sometimes more rage clings to a page than she would claim –
it's necessary to remain alert in letters

(an estranged friend donated to a library
three decades of her dishing out the dirt in letters)

and words which resonate and turn within
the mind can lie there flattened and inert in letters.

The tightest-laced precisely-spoken celibate
may inadvertently shrug off her shirt in letters.

Ex-lovers who won't lie down naked again
still permit themselves to flirt in letters.

What does Anonymous compose, unsigned
at night, after she draws the curtain? Letters.

Grief

Grief walks miles beside the polluted river,
grief counts days sucked into the winter solstice,
grief receives exuberant schoolyard voices
as flung despisals.

It will always be the first of September.
There will be Dominican boys whose soccer
game provides an innocent conversation
for the two people

drinking coffee, coatless. There will be sunset
roselight on the river like a cathedral.
There will be a rusty, amusing tugboat
pushing a barge home.

Did she think she knew what her friend intended?
Did she think her brother rejoiced to see her?
Did she think she'd sleep one more time till sunrise
holding her lover?

Grief has got no brother, sister or lover.
Grief finds friendship elsewhere. Grief, in the darkened
hours and hours before light flicks in one window
holds grief, a mirror.

Brother? He was dead, in a war-drained city.
Grief was shelling peas, with cold water running
in the sink; a harpsichord trilled Corelli
until the phone rang.

And when grief came home from a post-op nightwatch
two small girls looked reticent over homework.
Half the closet, half the drawers were empty.
Who was gone this time?

Grief is isolationist, short-viewed. Grief lacks
empathy, compassion, imagination;
reads accounts of massacres, floods and earthquakes
mired in one story.

Grief is individual, bourgeois, common
and banal, two women's exchange in Sunday
market: '*Le mari de Germaine est mort.*' They
fill bags with apples.

Grief is primagravida, in her fifth month.
Now she knows the fetus has died inside her.
Now she crosses shopping-streets on a sun-shot
mid-winter morning.

Winter licks the marrow from streets that open
onto parks and boulevards, rivers, river-
parallel parkways, arteries to bridges,
interstates, airports.

Grief daubs kohl on middle-aged burning eyelids.
Grief drives miles not noticing if the highway
runs beside an ocean, abandoned buildings
or blackened wheatfields

– and, in fact, she's indoors. Although her height is
average, massive furniture blocks and crowds her:
oak and pine, warm gold in their grain she thought would
ransom her season.

Workmen clear a path to repair the windows,
not with panes of light on their backs, no message-
bearers these. Still stubbornly green, a street leads
back to the river.

Fourteen years drained into the fifteen minutes
that it took a late-summer sun to douse its
light behind the opposite bank, the boys to
call their match over.

Migraine Sonnets

Entre chien et loup

It's a long way from the bedroom to the kitchen
when all the thought in back of thought is loss.
How wide the dark rooms are you walk across
with a glass of water and a migraine
tablet. Sweat of hard dreams: unforgiven
silences, missed opportunities.
The night progresses like chronic disease,
symptom by symptom, sentences without pardon.
It's only half past two, you realize.
Five windows are still lit across the street.
You wonder: did you tell as many lies
as it now appears were told to you?
And if you told them, how did you not know
they were lies? Did you know, and then forget?

There were lies. Did you know, and then forget
if there was a lie in the peach orchard? There was the lie
a saxophone riffed on a storm-thick summer sky,
there was the lie on a postcard, there was the lie thought
and suggested, there was the lie stretched taut
across the Atlantic, there was the lie that lay
slack in the blue lap of a September day,
there was the lie in bed, there was the lie that caught
its breath when it came, there was the lie that wept.
There was the lie that read the newspaper.
There was the lie that fell asleep, its clear
face relaxing back to the face of a child.
There was the lie you held while you both slept.
A lie hung framed in the doorway, growing wild.

The face framed in the doorframe is a wild
card now, mouth could eat silence, mouth could speak
the indigestible. Eyes, oh tourmaline, a crack
in the glass, break the glass. Down a green–tiled
corridor, double doors open. Who was wheeled
through, hallucinating on a gurney, weak
with relief as muscle and nerve flickered awake,
while a dreamed face framed in a doorframe opened and smiled?
Precisely no one's home. No dog will come
to lay his jowls across bent knees and drool
and smile the black-gummed smile he shares with wolves.
The empty doorframe frames an empty room
whose dim fluorescence is perpetual.
The double doors close back upon themselves.

The double doors close back upon themselves.
The watcher from the woods rejoins the pack:
shadows on branches' steely lacework, black
on black, dark ornaments, dark wooden shelves.
Fever-wolves, guardians a lamp dissolves
in pitiless logic, as an insomniac
waits to hear the long night crack and break
into contaminated rusty halves.
This is the ninety-seventh (count) night watch in
the underbrush of hours closed on you since
a lie split open like a rotten fruit.
A metal band around your head begins
to tighten; pain shutters your eyes like too much light.
It's a long way from the bedroom to the kitchen.

Explication de Texte

Plusieurs réponses sont possibles, mais montrez comment la ville peut
se lire comme un substitut de l'objet désiré
Text on Apollinaire for lycéens preparing the baccalauréat

> *Paris nights, drunk on gin,*
> *aflame with electrical fire.*
> *Trolleys with green-lit spines*
> *sing their long route down wire*
> *and rail, deranged machines.*
>> Guillaume Apollinaire, trans. M.H.

Paris is wintery gray.
The small rain spits and sputters.
Before the break of day
when green trucks hose the gutters
lights go on in the bakery.

The days go on, routine
light lingers on the clocks
Yellow and red and green
crowd in the window-box
impermanent and benign.

The tiny *sans-abri*
and her more substantial friend
arrive from a night on the quay
at their avenue, extend
their hands to earn their pay,

each on her opposite side.
They've been on the street together
for over a decade
while others jettisoned other
partners and promises made.

Bickering all the way
but punctual at their labors
weekday and holiday
they are my long-term neighbors
with Mme de Sévigné

The days go on, routine.
I would be happy never
to board another plane.
My feet, crossing the river,
and the La Défense/Vincennes

line, or Balard–Creteil
are forms of transportation
quite adequate for me.
Other communication
failed: well, let it be.

Sorrow becomes a sink
and loss becomes a drain.
The drain begins to stink.
Call the plumber again.
Remember how to think.

The poet who wrote and longed
for a woman he barely knew
by whom he thought he'd been wronged
gave Paris new verses to
her electrical torch-song:

the weedy, lovelorn merman's
complaint to pitiless sirens,
some similes, some sermons,
Montmartre and environs
– he even included Germans.

When friends say what they mean
companionship illumines
nights that unroll, routine
in being scaled for humans
choosing their food and wine.

We ordered a house *pichet*
and argued down to the wire at
a smoke-stained brown café:
my friend looked more like the pirate
than the pirate's fiancée.

Poached salmon followed soup
while another loquacious friend
talked such amazing shop
we left the 'Vagenende'
when the waiters were cleaning up.

Days and nights, routine
as unambiguous words:
accompanied, alone,
the hours are not like swords,
strike gently, like the rain.

I have two pairs of glasses:
for the peopled world beyond
the panes; for the small world this is
where I eat, and read *Le Monde*,
and drink, and the evening passes.

I grill my trout. I drink
three glasses of Brouilly
or some adequate Southwest plonk.
A Mozart symphony
drowns out the screech and honk

of buses, bikes and vans
and the selfsame garbage truck,
manned by green-clad Africans
come back at nine o'clock
to empty the big green cans.

Paris, elegant gray
godmother, consolation,
heartbroken lullaby,
smell of the métro station,
you won't abandon me.

A hot bath; Couperin:
the hours are not like swords,
strike gently, like the rain,
notes on a harpsichord
impermanent, benign.

On the Stairway

My fourth-floor neighbor, Mme. Uyttebroeck-
Achard, a widow in her seventies
wears champagne-froth lace sheaths above her knees
and patent-leather boots, and henna-red-
orange curls down to the white laminated
collar of her raincoat, like a striptease
artiste who's forgotten whom she needs to please.
She looks a lot like Violette Leduc.
On the dim stairway where she's paused and set
her shopping-bags down, the *aide-ménagère*
for Mme. Magin-Levacher, upstairs
one more flight, says Mme Uyttebroeck-Achard's '*pas nette*' –
not meaning 'clean,' but, in her dealings, 'clear'
– and I think of that muddy genius, Violette.

Quoi de neuf sur la guerre?

Café le Diplomate, Turenne / St.-Claude

Five old men
dissect last week's election.
Jacques' student granddaughter bought
a studio apartment

– bigger than
the three rooms that he lived in
with his two brothers, parents,
in the rue du Pont-aux-Choux...

(two streets up).
Glasses folded on his cap,
Maurice fishes for a not-
quite-lost riposte in Yiddish.

(His accent
is a familiar garment
on a neighbor, here or in
Strauss Park on upper Broadway.)

The senior
four worked here before the war.
Now they're back in the rag trade.
An eleven o'clock break

– tradition:
black coffee and discussion,
the *cheder* relived later.
The one two decades younger,

Victor, will
at last bring up Israel
– sixtyish son asking his
elders what ought to be done.

And Maurice,
the pouches around his eyes
creased deep in a sad smile, says,
having known wars, not much peace,

(a schoolboy
in Krakow in 1930)
'A solution? There is just
one. The final solution.'

Does he mean
the British had a plan in
'48: Arabs could finish
Hitler's job in the new state?

Does he mean
genocide in Palestine
to be practiced by 'our own'?
Victor changes the subject.

The waitress
interrupts exegesis:
Please pay, her shift is over.
The watchdog of the café,

a boxer,
trails his young boss, stops at her
trim heels. He scowls, sniffs the floor
and gets sawdust on his jowls.

Ghazal

She took what wasn't hers to take: desire
for all that's not her, for what might awake desire.

With it, the day's a quest, a question, answered where-
ever eye, mind lights. Desire seeks, but one can't seek desire.

A frayed wire, a proof, a flame, a drop of globed hot wax,
a riddle solved or not by William Blake: desire.

Erase the film with light, delete the files,
re-reel the story, will all that unmake desire?

For peace or cash, lovers and whores feign lust or climaxes.
A solitary can evoke, but cannot fake desire.

Crave nothing, accept the morning's washed and proffered air
brushing blued eyelids with an oblique desire.

There was an other, an answer, there was a Thou
or there were mutilations suffered for your sake, desire.

Without you, there is no poet, only some nameless hack
lacking a voice without your voice to speak desire.

Desesperanto

After Joseph Roth

Son service est plus propre à un estat trouble et malade comme est le nostre présent: vous diriez souvent qu'il nous peinct et qu'il nous pinse.
Montaigne, 'De l'art de conférer'

The dream's forfeit was a night in jail
and now the slant light is crepuscular.
Papers or not, you are a foreigner
whose name is always difficult to spell.
You pack your one valise. You ring the bell.
Might it not be prudent to disappear
beneath that mauve-blue sky above the square
fronting your cosmopolitan hotel?
You know two short-cuts to the train station
which could get you there, on foot, in time.
The person who's apprised of your intention
and seems to be your traveling companion
is merely the detritus of a dream.
You cross the lobby and go out alone.

You crossed the lobby and went out alone
through the square, where two red-headed girls played
hopscotch on a chalk grid, now in the shade,
of a broad-leafed plane tree, now in the sun.
The lively, lovely, widowed afternoon
disarmed, uncoupled, shuffled and disarrayed
itself; despite itself, dismayed
you with your certainties, your visa, gone
from your breast-pocket, or perhaps expired.
At the reception desk, no one inquired
if you'd be returning. Now you wonder why.
When the stout conductor comes down the aisle,
mustached, red-faced, at first jovial,
and asks for your passport, what will you say?

When they ask for your passport, will you say
that town's name they'd find unpronounceable
which resonates, when uttered, like a bell
in your mind's tower, as it did the day
you carried your green schoolbag down the gray
fog-cobbled street, past church, bakery, *shul*,
past farm women setting up market stalls
it was so early. 'I am on my way
to school in ——.' You were part of the town
now, not the furnished rooms you shared
with Mutti, since the others disappeared.
Your knees were red with cold; your itchy wool
socks had inched down, so you stooped to pull
them up, a student and a citizen.

You are a student and a citizen
of whatever state is transient.
You are no more or less the resident
of a hotel than you were of that town
whose borders were disputed and redrawn.
A prince conceded to a president.
Another language became relevant
to merchants on that street a child walked down
whom you remember, in the corridors
of cities you inhabit, polyglot
as the distinguished scholar you were not
to be. A slight accent sets you apart,
but it would mark you on that peddlers'-cart
street now. Which language, after all, is yours?

Which language, after all these streets, is yours,
and why are you here, waiting for a train?
You could have run a hot bath, read Montaigne.
But would footsteps beyond the bathroom door's
bolt have disturbed the nondescript interior's
familiarity, shadowed the plain
blue draperies? You reflect, you know no one
who would, of you, echo your author's
'*Because it was he; because it was I,*'
as a unique friendship's non sequitur.
No footsteps and no friend: that makes you free.
The train approaches, wreathed in smoke like fur
around the shoulders of a dowager
with no time for sentimentality.

With no time for sentimentality,
mulling a twice-postponed book-review,
you take an empty seat. Opposite you
a voluble immigrant family
is already unwrapping garlicky
sausages — an unshaven man and his two
red-eared sons.
                        You once wrote: it is true,
awful, and unimportant, finally,
that if the opportunity occurs
some of the exiles become storm-troopers;
and you try, culpably, to project these three
into some torch-lit future, filtering out
their wrangling (one of your languages) about
the next canto in their short odyssey.

The next canto in your short odyssey
will open, you know this, in yet another
hotel room. They have become your mother
country: benevolent anonymity
of rough starched sheets, dim lamp, rickety
escritoire, one window. Your neighbors gather
up their crusts and rinds. Out of a leather
satchel, the man takes their frayed identity
cards, examines them. The sons watch, pale
and less talkative. A border, passport control,
draw near: rubber stamp or interrogation?
You hope the customs officer lunched well;
reflect on the recurrent implication
of the dream's forfeit. One night in jail?

Morning News

Spring wafts up the smell of bus exhaust, of bread
and fried potatoes, tips green on the branches,
repeats old news: arrogance, ignorance, war.
A cinder-block wall shared by two houses
is new rubble. On one side was a kitchen
sink and a cupboard, on the other was
a bed, a bookshelf, three framed photographs.

Glass is shattered across the photographs;
two half-circles of hardened pocket-bread
sit on the cupboard. There provisionally was
shelter, a plastic truck under the branches
of a fig-tree. A knife flashed in the kitchen,
merely dicing garlic. Engines of war
move inexorably towards certain houses

while citizens sit safe in other houses
reading the newspaper, whose photographs
make sanitized excuses for the war.
There are innumerable kinds of bread
brought up from bakeries, baked in the kitchen:
the date, the latitude, tell which one was
dropped by a child beneath the bloodied branches.

The uncontrolled and multifurcate branches
of possibility infiltrate houses'
walls, windowframes, ceilings. Where there was
a tower, a town: ash and burnt wires, a graph
on a distant computer screen. Elsewhere, a kitchen
table's setting gapes, where children bred
to branch into new lives were culled for war.

Who wore this starched smocked cotton dress? Who wore
this jersey blazoned for the local branch
of the district soccer team? Who left this black bread
and this flat gold bread in their abandoned houses?
Whose father begged for mercy in the kitchen?
Whose memory will frame the photograph
and use the memory for what it was

never meant for by this girl, that old man, who was
caught on a ball-field, near a window: war,
exhorted through the grief a photograph
revives. (Or was the team a covert branch
of a banned group; were maps drawn in the kitchen,
a bomb thrust in a hollowed loaf of bread?)
What did the old men pray for in their houses

of prayer, the teachers teach in schoolhouses
between blackouts and blasts, when each word was
flensed by new censure, books exchanged for bread,
both hostage to the happenstance of war?
Sometimes the only schoolroom is a kitchen.
Outside the window, black strokes on a graph
of broken glass, birds line up on bare branches.

'This letter curves, this one spreads its branches
like friends holding hands outside their houses.'
Was the lesson stopped by gunfire? Was
there panic, silence? Does a torn photograph
still gather children in the teacher's kitchen?
Are they there meticulously learning war-
time lessons with the signs for house, book, bread?

Essay on Departure

And when you leave, and no one's left behind,
do you leave a cluttered room, a window framing
a zinc roof, other mansard windows? Do you
leave a row of sycamores, a river
that flows in your nocturnal pulse, a moon
sailing late-risen through clouds silvered by
the lights flung up from bridges? Do you leave
the wicker chairs the café owner stacks
at half-past-midnight while the last small clutch
of two girls and a boy smoke and discuss
what twenty-year-olds in cafés discuss
past midnight, with no war on here? You leave

the one and then the other, the all-night
eight-aisles-of-sundries with a pharmacy
cloned six times in one mile on upper Broadway.
Everywhere you're leaving something, leaving
no one, leaving as a season fades,
leaving the crisp anticipation of
the new, before its gold drops on the rain-
slick crossings to the walkways over bridges,
the schoolyard's newly painted *porte-cochère*:
remembered details. You're no longer there.
What's left when you have left, when what is left is
coins on the table and an empty cup?
An August lapse begins; the shutters drop
and lock, whatever follows is conjecture.
The sound feels final, punitive, a trap
shutting its jaws, though when the selfsame structure
was rolled up mornings, it was hopeful noise,
a reprieve from insomnia, a day's
presence opening possibility.
As you leave the place, you bring the time
you spent there to a closed parenthesis.
Now it is part of that amorphous past
parceled into flashes, slide-vignettes.
You'll never know if just what you forget's
the numinous and right detail, the key –
but to a door that is no longer yours,
glimpse of a morning-lit interior's
awakening silhouette, with the good blue
sky reflected on the tall blue walls,
then shadow swallows what was/wasn't true,
shutters the windows, sheathes the shelves in dust,
retains a sour taste and discards the kiss,
clings to the mood stripped of its narrative.
You take the present tense along. The place
you're leaving stops, dissolves into a past
in which it may have been, or it may not
have been (corroborate, but it's still gone)
the place you were, the moment that you leave.

NEW POEMS

Letter to Hayden Carruth

Dear Hayden, I have owed you a letter for
one month, or two – your last one's misplaced. But I'm
    back in New York. The world is howling,
    bleeding and dying in banner headlines.

No hope from youthful pacifists, elderly
anarchists; no solutions from diplomats.
    Men maddened with revealed religion
    murder their neighbors with righteous fervor,

while, claiming they're 'promoting democracy,'
our homespun junta exports the war machine.
    They, too, have daily prayer-meetings,
    photo-op-perfect for tame reporters.

('God Bless America' would be blasphemy
if there were a god concerned with humanity.)
    Marie is blunt about it: things were
    less awful (Stateside) in 1940.

I wasn't born… I've read shelves of books about
France under Vichy after the armistice:
    war at imagination's distance.
    Distance is telescoped now, shrinks daily.

Jews who learned their comportment from storm-troopers
act out the nightmares that woke their grandmothers;
    Jews sit, black-clad, claim peace: their vigil's
    not on the whistle-stop pol's agenda.

'Our' loss is grave: American, sacralized.
We are dismayed that dead Palestinians,
    Kashmiris, Chechens, Guatemalans,
    also are mourned with demands for vengeance.

'Our' loss is grave, that is, till a president
in spanking-new non-combatant uniform
    mandates a war: then, men and women
    dying for oil will be needed heroes.

I'd rather live in France (or live anywhere
there's literate debate in the newspapers).
    The English language is my mother
    tongue, but it travels. Asylum, exile?

You had New England; I had diaspora,
an old folk song: 'Wish I was where I would be,
    Then I'd be where I am not.' Would that
    joy claimed its citizens, issued passports.

'First, do no harm,' physicians, not presidents,
swear when inducted. I'm tired of rhetoric,
    theirs, journalists' or my own ranting.
    I'd like to hole up with Blake and Crashaw –

but there's a stack of student endeavors that
I've got to read, and write some encouraging
    words on. Five hours of class tomorrow;
    Tuesday, a dawn flight to California.

Glose

> Blood's risks, its hollows, its flames
> Exchanged for the pull of that song
> Bone-colored road, bone-colored sky
> Through the white days of the storm
>   Claire Malroux, 'Storm', trans. M.H.

Once out of the grip of desire,
or, if you prefer, its embrace,
free to do nothing more than admire
the sculptural planes of a face
(are you gay, straight or bi, are you *queer*?)
you still tell your old chaplet of names
which were numinous once, you replace
them with adjectives: witty, severe,
trilingual; abstracting blood's claims,
blood's risks, its hollows, its flames.

No craving, no yearning, no doubt,
no repulsion that follows release,
no presence you can't do without,
no absence an hour can't erase:
the conviction no reason could rout
of being essentially wrong
is dispelled. What feels oddly like peace
now fills space you had blathered about
where the nights were too short or too long,
exhanged for the pull of that song.

But peace requires more than one creature
released from the habit of craving
on a planet that's mortgaged its future
to the lot who are plotting and raving.
There are rifts which no surgeon can suture
overhead, in the street, undersea.
The bleak plain from which you are waving,
mapped by no wise, benevolent teacher
is not a delight to the eye:
bone-colored road, bone-colored sky.

You know that the weather has changed,
yet do not know what to expect,
with relevant figures expunged
and predictions at best incorrect.
Who knows on what line you'll be ranged
and who, in what cause, you will harm?
What cabal or junta or sect
has doctored the headlines, arranged
for perpetual cries of alarm
through the white days of the storm?

Glose

The rampart behind the leprosarium:
That also is Jerusalem.
Blue brooks cross the fields,
Light silver-leafs a stocky tree.

Emmanuel Moses, 'The Year of the Dragon',
trans. M.H.

Sunday noon haze on the fruit-stalls of Belleville,
a clochard's clothesline under the Pont des Arts,
the last Alsatian deli in the rue de Tourtille,
the second kosher couscous in the rue St.-Maur.
The Northern Line at midnight back from Stockwell
via Charing Cross, since no one, not even a cab, had come.
The Black Mountains lurching past a drunken car,
a mail-van threading the Col de Vence in lunar
dawn when the town's *enceinte* is a colombarium.
The rampart behind the leprosarium.

An equinoctial dusk wrapping the Square
du Temple; a hangnail moon glimpsed through light rain
on the Pont Sully; the 96 bus trapped by parked
motorcycles outside the Royal Turenne,
honking, while truck fumes mount, and the bus-driver
shouts at the *motards* what he thinks of them
somewhat distracting his stalled passengers
(the cyclists are pertinently not there);
the glass of water the waiter brings to him:
that also is Jerusalem.

Methods of crossing borders are diverse:
sixty years passed, and trains are innocent
again. Cream-colored cattle kneel; a lone horse
in a barnyard cocks a gray ear to the wind.
The sibilance of riverbanks, the terse
monosyllables a billboard holds
aloft above the tracks, a jet-trail's spent
calligraphy: their messages disperse
in the breached air whistling as it yields.
Blue brooks cross the fields.

ESSAYS ON DEPARTURE

In a vision of the perfected past,
a cindered path's circumference of vines
measures the play of words and breath, at last
conjoined in a few salvageable lines:
all of the hour's trajectory not lost
in burnt-out synapses of memory.
Yet some insight bestowed on aliens
inscribes the vineyard on a palimpsest
of city, valley, hills, a different city.
Light silver-leafs a stocky tree.

Ghazal: In Summer

for Mimi Khalvati

The air thickens, already more than half in summer.
At the corner café, girls in T-shirts laugh in summer.

The city streets, crowded with possibility
under spring rain, thin out, don't promise enough in summer.

That urge to write one's life instead of living it
makes sentences slip limply off-the-cuff in summer.

Slipped in a drawer under an expired passport,
curly-head in an orchard smiles for a photograph in summer.

Going downstairs early for bread: two winos snore on the landing,
'Can't they make do with sleeping in the rough in summer?'

Hard-case on the street, teacher out of class both harbor
a lowgrade fever and productive cough in summer.

Espresso winter, springtime of Juliénas:
black tea with honey's what I'll quaff in summer.

Despite my wall of books and Bach's geometries,
some scent wafts from the street to call my bluff in summer.

Not in a tank but a golf-cart rides the oligarch:
however, he does not dismiss his staff in summer.

Let them not, in Maryam's name or Marilyn's,
blot any cindered city off a graph in summer.

Letter to Mimi Khalvati

Dear, how I hate the overblown diction of
lines for occasions: festschrifts, like elegies
    making a banal birthday seem to
    signpost a passage to unmapped wasteland,

when thoughts and smiles are fresh as they've ever been
– at least my brief years given the privilege
    of bantering across some table,
    words made more fluent by cakes or curries

or by the short time left for exchanging them:
train in an hour, espresso in Styrofoam
    cups… Ciao! I wish… I'll tell you next time.
    Bus to the Eurostar, airport taxi.

I'll never see the light of your memories
(joy can be shared, but losses are separate)
    though we're a lucky pair of outcasts,
    free to embellish or keep our stories.

Yours, Mimi, silver's brilliance on velvety
shapes in the no-man's land between alphabets
    you were obliged to cross and cross to
    write in the white ink of exiled childhood.

Whose children *did* we talk about, smoking and
sipping Brouilly (an Indian family
    toasting some milestone near us) in the
    restaurant tucked behind Euston Station?

Two women, poised for middle-aged liberty,
still have our fledgling burdens to anchor us,
    wish they were soaring, independent,
        glad when they ground us with tea and gossip.

Think of the friendships lost to geography,
or lost to language, sex, or its absence... I
    send, crossing fingers, crossing water,
        bright thoughts, bright Maryam: happy birthday.

For Kateb Yacine

Algerian playwright, novelist, poet and activist, 1929–1989

A moment jumps the interval; the next
second, a sudden dissonance swells up,
a crack down the smooth surface of the cup,
a dialogue with mistranslated text,
a tense the narrative poises, perplexed,
upon. The dancers and the singer stop,
swirled, each, in shadow like a velvet cape,
potential, and ambiguously sexed.
A gender and a nationality
implicit in the ululation rise
from a long throat to claim or compromise
privilege; responsibility
in texture, in that wound of sound, that vexed
surface, which could detonate, could drop.

Could drop into the anonymity
of headlines: war and fear and fear of war
and war abetted by ambient fear
honed to a hunger by publicity.
But there is a room above the street, a three-
o'clock winter sun, the nuanced, nearly translucent voice of a counter-tenor
threading a cantata by Scarlatti.
There were the exile's words in Arabic

anathematizing any deity
if slaughter is sanctified in its name;
the voice, the struggle from which words became
corporeally transformed to music.
There is the emblematic cup of tea.

There is the emblematic pot of tea
steaming on a wooden bench between
antagonists engaged in conversation
halfway to official enmity,
halfway to some compromise they can agree
upon, and not lose face. A city drones
and screeches in the crepuscule beyond
the room, in contrapuntal energy.
They keep sentences moving, savor the way
to pluck the pertinent or flabby phrase
and skin and gut it, twisting in the air:
a game they magisterially play
like diplomats, not gray-sweatered, gray-haired
exiles filling the breach of winter days.

Exiles filling the breach of winter days
with rhetoric have nothing, but have time
for rhetoric as logical as rhyme.
Meanwhile a speechwriter drafts the ukase
which, broadcast to a military base,
sends children and their city up in flames.
Meanwhile, an editor collects our names
and texts in protest: we can only guess
who else is keeping tabs, who else will be
pilloried in an op-ed in the *Times*,
distracted by brief notoriety
or told a passport will not be renewed.
Imagined exiles, with what gratitude
I'd follow your riposted paradigms.

To make of his riposte a paradigm,
he conjured Nedjma from the wilderness
behind his distance-mined electric face.
Kahina, Nedjma, Amma, a woman's name
ejaculated to a stadium:
a heroine, a first lover unseen
for decades, a mother who mimed, silence upon

women's silence screamed past millennium.
Another silence, the interlocutor
who argued over wine with Paul Celan
until the words were not German or French
in the cold hypothesis of the Seine,
no longer comforter, companion, tutor
to the last Jew on the November bench.

If the last Jew on the November bench
shivered, rose, walked to the rue de Tournon
and ordered a Rémy and a *ballon*
de rouge with Roth, could it blot out the stench
of ash and lies for both? (Over the ranch
in Texas what smoke rises in premon-
itory pillar?) The gaunt Algerian
asynchronous, among them, needs to quench
an equal thirst. We all had pseudonyms,
code-names, pet-names, pen-names: *noms de guerre*,
simple transliterations, unfamiliar
diphthongs in rote order, palindromes
and puns patched on the untranslatable
(unuttered, anguished) root of a syllable.

Unuttered, anguished, roots of a syllable
in her first language threaded the page she'd sign
(written at night, in a strange town, hidden
among strangers, once betrayed) 'Nicole
Sauvage.'
          Sun gilds the roof of the town hall,
its bridal parties gone, too cold, too late.
The February sky is celibate,
precipitated towards a funeral.
Yes, war will come and we will demonstrate;
war will come and reams of contraband
reportage posted on the Internet
will flesh out censored stories, second-hand.
Tire-treads lumbering towards its already-fixed
moment jump the interval: this war, the next.

('Nicole Sauvage' was the pseudonym used by the writer Nathalie Sarraute
during the Nazi occupation of France during World War II, in the village
where she went into hiding with her daughters after being denounced as a
Jew by neighbors in another village.)

Glose

And I grew up in patterned tranquility
In the cool nursery of the new century.
And the voice of man was not dear to me,
But the voice of the wind I could understand.

Anna Akhmatova, 'Willow',
trans. Judith Hemschmeyer

A sibilant wind presaged a latish spring.
Bare birches leaned and whispered over the gravel path.
Only the river ever left. Still, someone would bring
back a new sailor middy to wear in the photograph
of the four of us. Sit still, stop *fidgeting*.
– Like the still-leafless trees with their facility
for lyric prologue and its gossipy aftermath.
I liked to make up stories. I liked to sing:
I was encouraged to cultivate that ability.
And I grew up in patterned tranquility.

In the single room, with a greasy stain like a scar
from the gas-fire's fumes, when any guest might be a threat
(and any threat was a guest – from the past or the future)
at any hour of the night, I would put the tea things out
though there were scrap-leaves of tea, but no sugar,
or a lump or two of sugar but no tea.
Two matches, a hoarded cigarette:
my day's page ashed on its bier in a bed-sitter.
No godmother had presaged such white nights to me
in the cool nursery of the young century.

The human voice distorted itself in speeches,
a rhetoric that locked locks and ticked off losses.
Our words were bare as that stand of winter birches
while poetasters sugared the party bosses'
edicts (the only sugar they could purchase)
with servile metaphor and simile.
The effects were mortal, however complex the causes.
When they beat their child beyond this thin wall, his screeches,
wails and pleas were the gibberish of history,
and the voice of man was not dear to me.

Men *and* women, I mean. Those high-pitched voices —
how I wanted them to shut up. They sound too much
like me. Little machines for evading choices,
little animals, selling their minds for touch.
The young widow's voice is just hers, as she memorizes
the words we read and burn, nights when we read and
burn with the words unsaid, hers and mine, as we watch
and are watched, and the river reflects what spies. Is
the winter trees' rustling a code to the winter land?
But the voice of the wind I could understand.

For Anna Akhmatova

Who had been in love with her that summer? Did it matter?
The incidental willow is what she would remember,
bare like a silver brooch on a sky of foxfur
during the winters of famine and deportations.
She wished she had something more cheerful to show them:
a list of the flowering shrubs in a city park,
lovers and toddlers asprawl behind rosebushes;
workers with mallets indulging in horseplay
while knocking partitions of sheetrock to splinters:
energy's avatars, feminine, masculine.
Forehead against the cold pane, she would always be
ten-and-a-half years older than the century.

★

She remembered Mother reading them Nekrasov
as they ate sardines with white cheese and tomatoes
while sun set late on the same seacoast where Tomis
had sheltered and repelled an exiled poet.
She would eat the same briny cheese in the heat of Tashkent
waiting for news from renamed Leningrad.

★

It had pleasured her, a language which incised
choreographed chance encounters, almost-uttered
words, eye-contact, electricity
of an evaded touch: she wrote about
brief summers, solitude's inebriation
in the dusk that fell at almost midnight.
(Louise Labé in a less clement climate,
with electricity and indoor plumbing.)
She and her friends and lovers chiselled lyrics
until the decade (what did they think of revolution?)
caught up with them, the elegant companions,
and set them to a different exercise.

★

(Which travelling companions would you pick?
Who would have chosen to endure Céline?
Pasternak wrote a paean to Stalin;
Donne, for Pascal, would be a heretic.)

★

Something held her back from choosing exile
when the exacting enterprise went rotten
Russia was not her motherland: it was St Petersburg,
the birch-lined corridors of Tsarskoye Selo –
but she was not retained by bark-scales spreading
up her limbs, with a god's breath in her ears: there
were her threatened friends, her son in prison
(who would not understand her coded letters
or what had held her back from choosing exile
after she did the paperwork to place him
in the Russian Gymnasium in Paris
the year his father met a firing squad;
and Marina – who would not live long –
wrote, she would meet them at the train station).
Tinned fish, gas rings, staggering armchairs, stained toilets
– mass graves of compromising manuscripts.
Was her exigent Muse the despised dictator
who censored, exiled, starved, imprisoned, murdered,
hurting the prodigy of birch and willow
into her late genius of debridement?
'Submissive to you? You must be out of your mind...'

★

How could she imagine, the '*gay little sinner*,' up
daybreak to dawn, the exactions of history?
City rerouted for transit to labor camps,
first husband shot in prison, their son in prison,
then in a labor camp, on the front, then still in prison.
She, over fifty, grown aquiline, vigilant,
larger than life, '*casta diva*,' her arias
camouflaged witness, evoking the dailiness
veiled in translation or foreign geographies.
Can you, yourself, in your eyrie, imagine it
while an empire's gearshifts creak behind you?

★

She made her despair the Virgin's or Cleopatra's
– under the circumstances, not outrageous.
She would write in praise of peace brought by the tyrant
if her lines might evoke an adjective passed down
from underling to underling until
some hungry guard unlocked a door... It didn't
happen. Her son called her superficial.
Larger than life, with all her flaws apparent
she rolled on the floor and howled in indignation,
more like the peasant she had come to resemble
than Anna Comnena or Cleopatra
or the ikon of words who was asked by other women
at the prison wall '*Can you describe this?*'

★

Once, in a youthful funk, she had made a poem of
her son (then just four), at her churchyard graveside
unable to resurrect his flighty mother
except to the balance sheet of her defections.
She was alone, and he was alive, in prison.
The impatient butterfly of Tsarskoye Selo
a solid matron, stood below the frozen
walls, with her permitted package, like the others –
whether they had been doting or neglectful mothers.

Ghazal: The Beloved

Remembering Faiz Ahmed Faiz

Lines that grapple doubt, written because of the beloved:
when grief subsides, what survives the loss of the beloved?

Your every declaration is suspect.
That was, at least, the departing gloss of the beloved.

Were you merely a servant of the state
or (now you give the coin a toss) of the beloved?

How pure you were, resistant in an orchard.
Peace with justice: the cause of the beloved.

A scent of hyacinth clings to your fingers,
of sap from a broken leaf, of moss, of the beloved.

Ambiguous predators howl within earshot.
You would like to curl up between the paws of the beloved.

Now uniforms cite scripture to erase you.
Only rabble and vermin die under the laws of the Beloved.

Who signed the warrant that sealed you in this cell?
Who read your messages? Who was the boss of the beloved?

How pure you were, how abject you are now,
waterboarded after the double-cross of the beloved.

You are promised release on the recognizance
(will this be a redemptive clause?) of the beloved.

Ghazal: Begin

The energy is mounting, something will, again, begin.
You will yourself to, know you will – but when – begin.

Remember anger. Remember indignation. Remember desire.
Feel that deceptive surge of adrenaline begin.

Select a rhyme, trust syntax for reason,
let rash conjuctions of the page and pen begin.

After the last postcard, last phonecall from home,
messages from somewhere beyond your ken begin.

Mathilde was eighteen. Arthur was seventeen.
One could see trouble in the ménage Verlaine begin.

Most of us first swooned in a woman's arms.
Where does that thralldom binding some to men begin?

Nights of champagne/cocaine pale into dawn.
Mornings of mint tea and Ibuprofen begin.

The doctor waking in a refugee camp
heard the keened lesssons of the gaunt children begin.

Lock Bush and Cheney up with Milosevic,
then let the trial of Saddam Hussein begin.

My brave friend's gone; our leaders are blindered bastards:
thus might an evening spent reading Montaigne begin.

As I poured that glass of wine, I thought of her
and felt the needlings of this damned migraine begin.

On the list I'm writing down of my addictions,
I'll let the oldest one, to oxygen, begin.

There where the fox was hungry, baffled, tired,
the tracks that led the hunters to his den begin.

Perhaps it will happen if you close your eyes
and count – but very slowly – backwards from ten. Begin.

Sháhid, if my name were Witness, I would sign it.
I leave when the tired jokes about 'Marilyn' begin.

Index of Titles

ESSAYS ON DEPARTURE

Index of First Lines